DOCE ME STATUTA TUA

BRADFIELD COLLEGE LIBRARY

E. M. FORSTER'S
HOWARDS END

FICTION AS HISTORY

TEXT AND CONTEXT

Editors

ARNOLD KETTLE
Professor of Literature
Open University

and

A. K. THORLBY
Professor of Comparative Literature
University of Sussex

◆

MICHAEL EGAN
Mark Twain's Huckleberry Finn:
Race, Class and Society

BERNARD HARRISON
Henry Fielding's Tom Jones:
The Novelist as Moral Philosopher

JEREMY HAWTHORN
Virginia Woolf's Mrs. Dalloway:
A Study in Alienation

DOUGLAS JEFFERSON
Jane Austen's Emma:
A Landmark in English Fiction

LAURENCE LERNER
Thomas Hardy's The Mayor of Casterbridge:
Tragedy or Social History?

PETER WIDDOWSON
E. M. Forster's Howards End:
Fiction as History

E. M. FORSTER'S
Howards End

FICTION AS HISTORY

Peter Widdowson

Thames Polytechnic

SUSSEX UNIVERSITY PRESS

1977

Published for
SUSSEX UNIVERSITY PRESS
by

Chatto & Windus Ltd
40 William IV Street
London WC2N 4DF
*
Clarke, Irwin & Co Ltd
Toronto

British Library Cataloguing in Publication Data
Widdowson, Peter
E. M. Forster's 'Howards End': fiction
as history. (Text and context).
Bibl.
ISBN 0-85621-067-6
ISBN 0-85621-068-4   Pbk
1. Title   2. Series
823'.9'12   PR6011.O58H6
Forster, Edward Morgan. Howards End

Printed in Great Britain by
Cox & Wyman Ltd,
London, Fakenham and Reading

CONTENTS

A NOTE ON TEXTS

I list below the books I refer to continuously, giving details of the edition used, and an abbreviated title for each. Page references to these works appear in brackets in the text, with the abbreviated title where necessary.

E. M. FORSTER

Abinger Harvest, (1936) (Edward Arnold 'Pocket Edition', 1946) **AH**

Aspects of the Novel, (1927) (Penguin Books, 1970) **AN**

Collected Short Stories, (1947) with Forster's Introduction (Penguin Books, 1969) **CSS**

Howards End, (1910) (Penguin Books, 1961) **HE**

Maurice, (1971) with Forster's Terminal Note and an Introduction by P. N. Furbank, (Penguin Books, 1975) **M**

Two Cheers for Democracy, (1951) (Penguin Books, 1972) **TC**

C. F. G. MASTERMAN

The Condition of England, (Methuen, 1909) **COE**

VIRGINIA WOOLF

'The Novels of E. M. Forster' in *Collected Essays*, Volume One (The Hogarth Press, 1966) **CE.I.**

ACKNOWLEDGEMENTS

The author and publishers wish to thank the following for permission to reproduce copyright material from the works of E. M. Forster: Sidgwick and Jackson for quotations from *Collected Short Stories* and Edward Arnold for quotations from the novels, essays and criticism.

1

INTRODUCTION: FICTION AS HISTORY

One interesting fact about *Howards End* is that it was written by 1910. It is, therefore, a product of that Indian summer of Victorian liberal-humanist culture which immediately preceded the First World War. At the same time, it is usually regarded as a 'modern novel', rather than Edwardian or Georgian. It seems, in some way, to be both an image of its own *milieu* and symptomatic of subsequent developments, a creation 'Wandering between two worlds, one dead, /The other powerless to be born'.[1] The novel in fact contains both an ardent affirmation of liberal-humanist values and an intuition of their vulnerability - perhaps their inefficacy - in the process of contemporary social change. Nevertheless, both in structure and idea, *Howards End*, written before 'the world broke up' in 1914 (*TC*.305), just manages to resist the depredations of those 'decivilizing' forces which Forster sensed in the modern world, and finally postulates the survival of the values he cherished. The victory, however, was Pyrrhic.

Howards End, like all fiction, is history; not, of course, history as a more or less direct rendering of factual evidence, but as itself a part of the historical process, which contains and reveals the pressures of social and cultural change. Fiction does not simply *reflect* its times. It expresses them, rather, in a complex synthesis which cannot be defined solely in terms of 'subject-matter' or 'ideas', a synthesis in which all the given material is fused and transformed within its particular form. As Forster himself put it: 'the novel's success lies in its own sensitiveness, not in the success of its subject matter'. (*AN*.27) To make a distinction, of course, between material and its form would be to disintegrate the total 'statement' which any novel makes. The importance of regarding the text as an organic structure becomes more readily apparent if the relationship between fiction and society is analysed a stage further.

By its nature, fiction is a form of rhetoric: it has to convince the reader of its reality. All its formal structures and devices are employed to this end. As Forster, again, has variously put it: the writer 'when he is inventing truly . . . . floats us over improbabilities' (AN.61); or rather he must possess 'the valuable faculty of faking'. (CSS.6) The rhetoric of fiction, in other words, is primarily concerned to make the world it creates *seem real*, at least *within* each individual novel's terms of reference and whether it be thriller, social novel, historical novel, Gothic novel, science fiction or any other mode. Whatever the nature and origin of the raw material a novel draws on, it does not merely ingest material from the society in which it is written, dissolve and recreate it; it also transmits its world *outwards*. Its synthetic statement is projected, as successfully as possible, *into* society and its success is entirely dependent on the efficacy of its formal expression. To read fiction as history therefore, in terms of subject-matter alone is to engage in a futile and reductive activity. Novels are not passively or reflexively historical; they are actively so, creating forms of the world within themselves which may well modify consciousness in the world outside. The relationship between fiction and society, then, is complex, inter-active and dynamic. And *Howards End* is an excellent example of it.

But what kind of historical understanding does a novel offer, given the insistent control of its particular form and the tendency to 'fake'? At various points in his career, Forster himself has presented some oblique clues to the nature of fiction as history. In an essay called 'The Consolations of History' (1920), he lightheartedly suggests that one should get *inside* history, circumventing the inaccessibility of the 'great figures', and discover the ordinariness of the life of the past:

> Difficult to realise that the past was once the present, and that, transferred to it, one would be just the same little worm as today, unimportant, parasitic, nervous, occupied with trifles, unable to go anywhere or alter anything, friendly with the obscure, and only at ease with the dead; while up on the heights the figures and forces who make History would contend in their habitual fashion, with incomprehensible noises or in ominous quiet. (AH.163)

It is not particularly surprising, in the light of this, that Forster should have admired the exposures of private life offered by

Lytton Strachey's historical works. In the essay 'English Prose Between 1918 and 1939', he offers some significant remarks about Strachey's approach:

> Lytton Strachey makes his people move; they are alive like characters in a novel: he constructs or rather reconstructs them from within. Sometimes he got them wrong . . . . But even when they are wrong they seem alive, and in the *Queen Victoria* his facts have not been seriously challenged; and, based on dry documents, a whole society and its inhabitants rise from the grave and walk about. That was his great contribution. He was a historian who worked from within, and constructed out of the bones of the past something more real and more satisfactory than the chaos surrounding him. (*TC.* 285-6)

Disregarding Forster's evaluation of Strachey's historical accuracy, and idiosyncratic final comment, two connected points of interest remain: first that Strachey constructs or reconstructs characters from within *like a novelist*, and second, that he was 'a historian who worked from within'. Strachey, in other words, is like a novelist who creates a world which is alive, even if it has no direct correlation with the actual facts of life; it is, to borrow another of Forster's own formulations, 'convincing', although not 'real'. (*AN.* 68-9) The implicit and concomitant idea that the novelist himself is an historian who works from within, is made clearer if we turn to Forster's comparison of fiction and history in *Aspects of the Novel.*

The fact is, however, that the basis of his approach in this book is explicitly ahistorical, and this helps to explain the type of historian the novelist is. He speaks of the need 'to exorcise that demon of chronology' (21), and posits all the novelists he is dealing with as 'seated together in a room, a circular room, a sort of British Museum reading-room - all writing their novels simultaneously.' (16) But this is consequent on Forster's attempt, here, to isolate and describe the basic components of the novel form, and it leads to his distinction between History and Fiction, in terms of character:

> If a character in a novel is exactly like Queen Victoria - not rather like but exactly like - then it actually is Queen Victoria, and the novel, or all of it that the character touches, becomes

a memoir. A memoir is history, it is based on evidence. A novel is based on evidence + or − x, the unknown quantity being the temperament of the novelist, and the unknown quantity always modifies the effect of the evidence, and sometimes transforms it entirely.

The historian deals with actions, and with the characters of men only so far as he can deduce them from their actions. He is quite as much concerned with character as the novelist, but he can only know of its existence when it shows on the surface. . . . The hidden life is, by definition, hidden. The hidden life that appears in external signs is hidden no longer, has entered the realm of action. And it is the function of the novelist to reveal the hidden life at its source: to tell us more about Queen Victoria than could be known, and thus to produce a character who is not the Queen Victoria of history. (52-3)

Forster's main point here is that the novelist enters a dimension of experience which historians cannot penetrate, and he goes on to say that, in a novel, the characters' 'inner as well as their outer life can be explored'. (54) At the end of the same chapter, Forster makes his logical claim:

In this direction fiction is truer than history, because it goes beyond the evidence, and each of us knows from his own experience that there is something beyond the evidence . . . (70)

If we take these remarks together with those on Lytton Strachey, Forster's basic position appears to be that the novelist is an historian working from within, an historian, in some sense, of the hidden or inner, life.

Leaving aside for the time being what Forster may mean by the 'inner life', his comments are helpful in defining what the concept of 'fiction as history' implies. History is fundamentally concerned with causality and change, and as a consequence it normally moves on a horizontal plane, dealing with the acted, public expression of infinitely complex situations. Thomas Carlyle, in an early essay, 'On History', defines the tendencies of written history by saying that it is 'narrative', and that 'Narrative is *linear*; Action is *solid*'; that beneath any *sequence* of events is a 'Chaos of Being' in which innumerable factors are operative *simultaneously*, not *successively* as in linear narrative progression.[2]

10

It is this hidden Action, I suggest, which fiction helps to reveal. Novels cut vertically across the linear narrative of history to produce images of 'solid Action'. They attempt to create solid sections of individual human existence which will contain the private or inner explanations of public, historical, situations. The novelist, by the nature of his form, is primarily concerned with individual experience - with the hidden, inner life, of his characters - but this may well be symptomatic of much more general states of being. This is one sense in which fiction may be regarded as history from within.

But novels are also products of an historically-placed consciousness: the author's, and that too will have been moulded by the society in which he exists. A novel creates a world which *reveals* (although the author may simply be attempting to reflect or describe) a view of the 'real' world at a particular point in time. This is not to say that a novel is merely a conscious expression of the author's world-view, but that the novel's created world itself represents a world-view with all its - often unperceived - tensions, contradictions and exclusions. This is 'history from within' at the second level: novels contain social configurations solidly realised in all their structures, and thus immediately become 'history'; not the history of public events, but the inner history of the 'Chaos of Being' which engenders them.

There are, then, two principal expressions of history from within in a novel, one tending to be conscious and intentional, the other tending to be unconscious and unintentional. The first is that of the author attempting to define a condition of life through the action, characterisation and created texture of his work. This may be described crudely as the theme and pattern of a book. In the case of *Howards End*, I shall indicate how Forster attempts to realise a particular cultural situation in the characters of Margaret and Helen Schlegel especially, and in the action which is used to define them: that they are, for Forster himself, 'representative images' as well as 'characters'. The second case, however, is less straightforward. There is, as I have said, a fundamental correlation between an author's world-view and his formal expression. A novelist's use of plot, of verbal rhetoric, of contingency, of symbolism, his manipulation of character, his shifting narrative point-of-view, his more or less obtrusive 'faking', will reveal uncertainties and ambivalences in his view of life

11

that informs the world of the novel. It is in its gaps, contradictions, tensions and 'structural faults' that a novel is, at the second level, history from within. But here it is the reader, rather than the author, who may perceive the hidden life of the past: the novel *itself* contains and reveals the logic of its world in the literary structures by which that world has been built. Here, to borrow D. H. Lawrence's famous remark, one 'trusts the tale' rather than 'the artist'.

Once again *Howards End* offers an excellent illustration of this. Ambivalence is a crucial factor in Forster's work, and in *Howards End* in particular there is an ambivalence which is both intentional and unintentional, structural and ideological. Even the epigraph - 'Only connect . . .' - itself implies these ambivalences. Normally read as Forster's positive imperative: 'All we must do is connect', it suggests too the plaintive, despairing tones of a fading faith: 'If only we could connect . . .'. And, concurrent with such ideological connotations, the phrase also identifies the structural tendency of the novel: connective, resolving, synthetic. *Howards End* operates, then, at both levels of 'history from within': *Forster* (the artist) describes a situation (the need to 'connect') and resolves it in terms of a particular set of values; *the novel itself* (the tale) suggests now, to us, the unresolved tension between situation and values. *Howards End* reveals, in other words, that its own connections may be suspect.

It is perhaps worth remarking here, in order to avoid future confusion, that it is precisely in the tensions, irresolutions and ambiguities of the novel that its strength resides. Whatever the flaws, weaknesses and contradictions we may perceive in Forster's own ideological position, the novel, by containing them, gains rather than loses. Otherwise we would be demanding that fiction should be polemical, a prosaic exposition of views or ideas, rather than the densely textured recreation of the world as it is perceived by one who is an individual product of a larger social consciousness. The rich ambiguity, the fundamental *irresolution* of *Howards End* are key factors in its importance as a novel; it is they, as much as anything else, which help it constantly and dynamically to enact a part of the past for the present.

But what precisely is the 'history' that the novel contains? In what contexts is the novel to be read? *Howards End* reveals two interrelated crises. Firstly, it registers, at both of our levels, important symptoms of the crisis of liberalism and liberal-humanism in the 20th century. This it does both historically and prophetically; by which I mean that it is organically related to its own time and place, but at the same time anticipates a tendency which is intensified in subsequent decades. I shall elaborate this 'context' more fully in the following sections, here I merely wish to state my themes. The liberal crisis has been tellingly defined by Raymond Williams in an essay on Ibsen in *Modern Tragedy*. Having explained how the liberal individual has, by the end of the 19th century, identified his true enemy as Society, although his fundamental drive is to be an organic part of it, Williams continues:

> Certainly there is to be reform, the 'sick earth' is to be 'made whole', but this is to happen, always, by an individual act: the liberal conscience, *against* society. Change is never to be *with* people; if others come they can at most be led. But also change, significantly often, is against people; it is against their wills that the liberator is thrown, and disillusion is then rapid. He speaks for human desire, as a general fact, but he knows this only as individual fulfilment. . . . . . It is the final tragic recognition: that the self, which is all that is known as desire, leads away from fulfilment, and to its own breakdown.
>
> From this recognition, there is no way out, within the liberal consciousness. There is either the movement to common desire, common aspiration, which politically is socialism, or there is acceptance, reluctant at first but strengthening and darkening, of failure and breakdown as common and inevitable.[3]

What Forster attempts in *Howards End* is to establish a defensive position through individual 'connection', against the breakdown he already senses but does not fully comprehend before the First World War. 'Failure and breakdown', although courageously held at bay, is the insistent undertone of his post-war writings, in *A Passage to India* and in most of the essays in *Abinger Harvest* and *Two Cheers for Democracy*. But it is the attempt in *Howards End* to create the idea of 'community' within the liberal value system, while recognising the hostile realities of the world it is to 'make whole', that causes strains and tensions in the novel itself. A vision of what the world should be, not what it is, has to be imposed on the novel to make it affirmative, and this creates significant tensions when combined with more 'realistic' observations.

And this points to the second 'crisis'; one which *Howards End* identifies but which Forster, at the time, scarcely recognised: that of the realistic novel itself in the 20th century. The English realist tradition, essentially a product of the middle-class liberal imagination has, with certain important exceptions, assumed that there is a palpable 'outside world' with commonly accepted features which it was its task to describe and pattern in order to reveal significance. Hence the constant pursuit of verisimilitude, and the use of 'faking' on its behalf. But in the 20th century, as the sense of a commonly received world fragmented, so too did the adequacy of conventional realism. 'Vision', 'fabulation', 'fantasy' and other non-realistic modes began to intrude, offering routes for withdrawal, hopeful solutions for the future, or, more usually, dreadful visions of a hell which circumscribes us here. David Lodge, in his essay 'The Novelist at the Crossroads', has well described the later manifestations of this crisis. The realistic novel, he explains, has held 'history, romance and allegory together in precarious synthesis', and 'supremely among literary forms has satisfied our hunger for the meaningful ordering of experience *without* changing our empirical observation of its randomness and particularity.' But, he continues, under the pressures of modern society 'the common phenomenal world' recedes, and 'the writer finds himself in a region of myths, dreams, symbols and archetypes that demand "fictional" rather than "empirical" modes for their expression'.[4] 'Fictional modes', in uneasy relationship with 'empirical' realism, are one of the symptoms in *Howards End* of the insecurity of the liberal-realist hegemony, which the following decades of the 20th century were to make more acute.

'Fantasy', of a light and traditionally-warranted kind, had of course always been to Forster's taste - I shall return to this later - and his short stories, all written before 1914, he has himself called 'fantasies'. But his 1947 introduction to the *Collected Short Stories* shows a significant awareness of what had happened in the meantime:

Much has happened since: transport has been disorganised,

frontiers rectified on the map and in the spirit, there has been a second world war, there are preparations for a third, and Fantasy today tends to retreat or to dig herself in or to become apocalyptic out of deference to the atom-bomb. She can be caught in the open here [in his stories] by those who care to catch her. She flits over the scenes of Italian and English holidays, or wings her way with even less justification towards the countries of the future. (*CSS.* 5)

In *Howards End* a type of fantasy is apparent at times, but not of the light, intrinsically irresponsible kind Forster suggests here. Fantasy has become a device for affirming an uncertain social vision against the logic of more 'empirical' perceptions. And it is here, of course, that the two 'crises' intersect: the world can no longer be 'realistically' *described* without exposing the inefficacy of liberal-humanist values, therefore the world has to be *remade*, by fictional contrivance, to accommodate them. Verisimilitude, in other words, gives way to a type of fabulation as the world and the vision diverge. Before 1914, faith in the liberal-humanist vision could still be affirmed, even though it was seriously threatened and it could still be presented *as if* empirically observed, despite the need to deploy contrived or 'fabulous' modes in order to give it substance. But the explicit correlation between liberal despair - 'failure and breakdown' - and the inadequacy of empirical realism belongs to the post-war period: 'an age', says Forster, 'in which sensitive people could not feel comfortable, and were driven to seek inner compensation'; an age in which modern writers 'look outside them and find their material lying about in the world. But they arrange it and re-create it within, temporarily sheltered from the pitiless blasts and the fog.' (*TC* 284) And in 1920, apostrophising a 'fantasy' - 'O beautiful book! O wisest of books!' - Forster reveals his own disaffection with the world and, implicitly, with a mode which attempted to describe it:

In the heart of each man there is contrived, by desperate devices, a magical island such as yours. We place it in the past or the future for safety, for we dare not locate it in the present . . . We call it a memory or a vision to lend it solidity, but it is neither really; it is the outcome of our sadness, and of our disgust with the world that we have made. (*AH.* 38)

15

Two years later, after *A Passage to India* was published (it had been started before the war), Forster stopped writing novels altogether.

These are the broad 'contexts' in which *Howards End* is most fruitfully read, and the following sections will suggest more fully their nature and characteristics. But just as it is imperative to see the text in context, so it is to perceive that the text *contains* its context, and the subsequent detailed analysis of the novel is intended to do exactly that. However, it is as well before we discuss the 'external' contexts, at least to *locate* them within the text, so that the complex relationship of fiction and society does not become a crude and disjunctive placing of text *against* its background. To do this I will take one fairly long, but not particularly explicit, passage from the novel, and illustrate how context permeates text.

The introductory paragraphs, at the beginning of Chapter XIII, introduce the action which develops two years after Mrs Wilcox's death. They describe London and the Schlegels' relationship to it:

> Over two years passed, and the Schlegel household continued to lead its life of cultured but not ignoble ease, still swimming gracefully on the grey tides of London. Concerts and plays swept past them, money had been spent and renewed, reputations won and lost, and the city herself, emblematic of their lives, rose and fell in a continual flux, while her shallows washed more widely against the hills of Surrey and over the fields of Hertfordshire. This famous building had arisen, that was doomed. To-day Whitehall had been transformed: it would be the turn of Regent Street to-morrow. And month by month the roads smelt more strongly of petrol, and were more difficult to cross, and human beings heard each other speak with greater difficulty, breathed less of the air, and saw less of the sky. Nature withdrew: the leaves were falling by midsummer; the sun shone through dirt with an admired obscurity.
>
> To speak against London is no longer fashionable. The Earth as an artistic cult has had its day, and the literature of the near future will probably ignore the country and seek inspiration from the town. One can understand the reaction. Of Pan and the elemental forces, the public has heard a little

too much - they seem Victorian, while London is Georgian - and those who are for the earth with sincerity may wait long ere the pendulum swings back to her again. Certainly London fascinates. One visualizes it as a tract of quivering grey, intelligent without purpose, and excitable without love; as a spirit that has altered before it can be chronicled; as a heart that certainly beats, but with no pulsation of humanity. It lies beyond everything: Nature, with all her cruelty, comes nearer to us than do these crowds of men. A friend explains himself: the earth is explicable - from her we came, and we must return to her. But who can explain Westminster Bridge Road or Liverpool Street in the morning - the city inhaling - or the same thoroughfares in the evening - the city exhaling her exhausted air? We reach in desperation beyond the fog, beyond the very stars, the voids of the universe are ransacked to justify the monster, and stamped with a human face. London is religion's opportunity - not the decorous religion of theologians, but anthropomorphic, crude. Yes, the continuous flow would be tolerable if a man of our own sort - not anyone pompous or tearful - were caring for us up in the sky.

The Londoner seldom understands his city until it sweeps him, too, away from his moorings, and Margaret's eyes were not opened until the lease of Wickham Place expired. She had always known that it must expire, but the knowledge only became vivid about nine months before the event. Then the house was suddenly ringed with pathos. It had seen so much happiness. Why had it to be swept away? In the streets of the city she noted for the first time the architecture of hurry, and heard the language of hurry on the mouths of its inhabitants - clipped words, formless sentences, potted expressions of approval or disgust. Month by month things were stepping livelier, but to what goal? The population still rose, but what was the quality of the men born? The particular millionaire who owned the freehold of Wickham Place, and desired to erect Babylonian flats upon it - what right had he to stir so large a portion of the quivering jelly? He was not a fool - she had heard him expose Socialism - but true insight began just where his intelligence ended, and one gathered that this was the case with most millionaires. What right had such men - But Margaret checked herself. That way lies madness. Thank

17

goodness she, too, had some money, and could purchase a new home. (*HE*.102-3)

The first point to notice is the disaffection Forster feels for London, and for London as in some sense symptomatic of a whole new way of life. The encroachment of suburbia on the countryside (an important late Victorian and Edwardian development) is part of this: 'her shallows washed more widely against the hills of Surrey and over the fields of Hertfordshire'. So too is the sense of persistent change - buildings rising and falling - and the unnatural, unhealthy bustle of the inhabitants' life: 'And month by month the roads smelt more strongly of petrol, and were more difficult to cross. . . .' etc. The Schlegels' existence is involved in this: the city was 'emblematic of their lives'. Living in London, they are part of it and dance to its rhythms. Nevertheless, Margaret, who is Forster's main proponent of liberal-humanist values in the novel, is herself disenchanted by the life of which she is a part: 'In the streets of the city she noted for the first time the architecture of hurry, and heard the language of hurry on the mouths of its inhabitants. . . . Month by month things were stepping livelier, but to what goal? The population still rose, but what was the quality of the men born?' Here, then, at one and the same time, is a perception of a new society developing, of which people cannot fail to be a part, and a strong sense of alienation from it, revealed in Margaret's tones of fastidious distaste. (In fact, as I shall show, they are Forster's too.) And such cultural alienation is, as Raymond Williams suggested, a key experience in the liberal crisis. But this perception contains another perception within it which is crucial to it: that there has been another type of life which is superior to the one developing. This, as the passage implies, belongs to the past and to 'the Earth'. There is, therefore, the 'civilization' of modern London rudely superceding the passing civilization of rural England. Quite clearly Forster's sympathies are with the latter, since London is merely 'a tract of quivering grey, intelligent without purpose, and excitable without love'. This inclination to look back to the rural past, to the 'organic community', is also, as we shall see, a feature of liberal alienation from modern society. Nevertheless, Forster recognises, and this in itself is symptomatic of the liberal dilemma, that such attitudes are *passé*, out-moded: 'To speak against

18

London is no longer fashionable. The Earth as an artistic cult has had its day, and the literature of the near future will probably ignore the country and seek inspiration from the town'. Such ambivalent perceptions represent both the triumph and the failure of the liberal position.

Further significant ambivalences are apparent in the passage. Despite London being 'emblematic of their lives', the Schlegels live a life of 'cultured *but not ignoble* ease'. And Margaret, as we have seen, questions the quality of life which London engenders. She is also able to recognise that 'true insight began just where his [the property millionaire's] intelligence ended'. Implicit, then, in the Schlegels', and particularly Margaret's, values lies some hope for civilization, and this, as we shall see, the novel goes on to affirm. However, it is also apparent that a life of values such as hers is dependent on a material base which the despised millionaire has in common with it - money: 'Thank goodness she, too, had some money, and could purchase a new home.' Forster recognises the crucial factor in the liberal dilemma: that values cannot survive without secure financial support, 'money', as he remarks at the beginning of the passage, which 'had been spent and *renewed*'. The economic base of liberalism poses awkward questions for the liberal sensibility committed to justice and culture. The whole passage, therefore, expresses the sense of a rapidly changing society at the beginning of the century, the fear and dislike which this brings with it, and at the same time the understanding, but not acceptance, that one is organically related to it. It is the classic liberal paradox of wishing to be a part, but apart.

We might further note, in passing, that Forster also senses a radical change in literary attitudes: 'The Earth as an artistic cult has had its day' etc., although his ironic tone slightly qualifies the certainty of the proposition. But what is more noteworthy is his use of generalised 'literary' idiom to define what he regrets is passing: 'Pan and the elemental forces'. 'Pan' had already featured as a life-force in some of Forster's earlier 'fantasies', and his presence here suggests something of the mystical or visionary quality of the values Forster would oppose to the reality of 'London'. The 'unseen', as Forster calls it elsewhere, is notoriously difficult to express in other than vague and heightened language - which possibly implies the weakness of the vision in terms of concrete social realisation. But we should also notice that even 'London' in this passage (especially in the second paragraph) is described in highly rhetorical prose: 'We reach in desperation beyond the fog, beyond the very stars, the voids of the universe are ransacked to justify the monster, and stamped with a human face.' It is as though the super-real horror of London defies Forster to comprehend its reality in denotative terms. A movement between 'realistic' specificity and generalising rhetoric (especially at points when 'realism' is inapposite or inadequate) is characteristic of the novel as a whole, and bears witness to its uncertainty of mode. Forster's apprehension of the crisis confronting his world, the forces of destruction and the forces of salvation, often seems to be beyond the scope of realism. And one may add that just as Forster's own tentativeness, his irony, self-consciousness and self-criticism, represent a maturity of perception and understanding, so too does the complex ambivalence of the novel's structures comprise its vitality.

A single passage from *Howards End*, then, contains within it suggestions of the 'contexts' in which the novel is situated. It is to some consideration of these *outside* the novel that we must now turn.

'THE CONDITION OF ENGLAND', 1900-14

Howards End was published in 1910 - the year Edward VII died. It falls foursquare, therefore, in the middle of that holding period, 'between two worlds', which the fourteen years from Queen Victoria's death to the Great War now seem to have been. It falls four years on from the Liberal landslide victory of 1906, and right at the start of that four-year period which, for George Dangerfield at least, witnesses 'the strange death of Liberal England'.[1] It appeared the year following C. F. G. Masterman's widely-read analysis of the state of the age, *The Condition of England* (1909). Masterman's book in itself offers an interesting 'context' for Forster's novel,[2] and I shall keep returning to it as a way of explaining how integral to its time *Howards End* is. Masterman was on the radical wing of the Liberal Party and was M.P. for two East London constituencies during the period. His analysis of contemporary England reflects his position: both his sense of the need for a radical programme for the Liberal Party, and his underlying uncertainty about the security of Liberal England. As with Forster, there is a prophetic sense of the crisis, especially at the level of threatened values; and it is within this frame of reference that his analysis of 'the condition of England' is undertaken. The similarity of their position is at times uncanny, and to place Forster within the contemporary ambience of liberal social criticism, it is helpful to glance at some of Masterman's attitudes. He, too, has a profound sense of the conflict between the old life and the new; and London for him, as for Forster, seems symbolic of the new urban existence: 'this monster clot of humanity' is 'breeding . . . a special race of men'. (*COE*.99). And he describes it in significant terms:

> Divorced from the ancient sanities of manual or skilful labour, of exercise in the open air, absorbed for the bulk of his day in crowded offices adding sums or writing letters, each a unit in a crowd which has drifted away from the realities of life in a complex, artificial city civilization, he comes to see no other

universe than this - the rejoicing over hired sportsmen who play before him, the ingenuities of sedentary guessing competitions, the huge frivolity and ignorance of the world of the music hall and the Yellow newspaper. (94)

A note of hysteria may seem to be an inevitable accompaniment of a city life so divorced from the earth's ancient tranquillity as never to appear entirely sane. And the future of the city populations, ever 'speeded up' by more insistent bustles and noises and nervous explosions, takes upon itself, in its normal activities, something hitherto abnormal to humanity. (124)

Not only does he despise the speed, artificiality and triviality of city life, much as Forster does in the passage we looked at above, but he also posits 'the earth' and the 'ancient sanities' of rural life as basic values. Indeed, later on, Masterman sees the only hope for the future in such values: 'This unquestioning love of the Earth and the children of it is perhaps the most hopeful element for future progress.' (256) This statement, as we shall see, is almost exactly parallelled by the ending of *Howards End*. Nevertheless, despite the hope, Masterman is aware of the destructive process. The continuous undertone of his book is 'rural England crumbling into ruin' (29), 'rural England . . . everywhere hastening to decay' (190), 'the vanishing of [the] "yeoman" class' (82); and it is significant in the context of *Howards End*, that one of his iterative motifs of destruction is the motor car of the wealthy: 'you can see the evidence of their activity in the dust-laden hedges of the south country roads, a grey mud colour, with no evidence of green; in the ruined cottage gardens of the south country villages.' (207) Forster describes Charles Wilcox's 'activity' in almost precisely the same terms at the beginning of *Howards End*. (see *HE*.19)

In addition to this characteristically dual perception of 'rural England', Masterman's fundamental humanist values are almost identical to Forster's: he too clearly regards 'Tolerance, kindliness, sympathy, civilization' (266), as fundamental to life; he too seeks 'satisfaction in quietness and common things - the untroubled horizon, the secure possession of the heart of humanity' (221); he too loathes the 'increased hustling and speeding up of human life; more hurry, more bustle, more breathlessness, more triumphant supremacy of material things.' (218) All of which statements could be parallelled time and again in Forster's writings. But like Forster once more, Masterman is aware of the paradox at the heart of liberalism, the dependence of its values on a secure economic base; and he warns that 'Delirium' will follow if 'liberal' society forgets 'the conditions of labour and service upon which alone that security can be maintained.' (29) *The Condition of England*, then, suggests something of the liberal-humanist ethos, before the Great War, in which *Howards End* was written.

But what Masterman's book primarily perceives and expresses is the sense of the contemporary world poised on the edge of massive and radical change. What form it is to take Masterman does not know:

> We can find no answer to the inquiry, whether we are about to plunge into a new period of tumult and upheaval, whether we are destined to an indefinite prolongation of the present half-lights and shadows, whether, as we sometimes try to anticipate, a door is to be suddenly opened, revealing unimaginable glories. (304)

Uncertainty about the development of the world informs Forster's position, too, before the war, but for a liberal-humanist intellectual in 1909, hope just overcomes fear. Nevertheless, the fear persists; and Masterman, like Thomas Carlyle who had written about 'the Condition of England' a couple of generations earlier, offers a warning to his complacent contemporaries that they should at least understand the nature of their world if they are to make it survive. This society, he wrote, 'will pass, if it passes, . . . because an unwillingness to face reality is gradually developing a confusion between reality and illusion; because in its prosperity, it may be stricken blind to the signs of the times.' (67) This further echo of Carlyle is not fortuitous: what Masterman offers, and implies others should engage in too, is an analysis of the age so that the imminence of change is recognised:

> For two hundred and fifty years ten generations have flourished and faded in a universe where regular government and an ordered apparatus of justice have guaranteed that life shall be reasonably safe, and that foresight shall attain reward. . . . Yet during the whole of this period there have been cataclysms of change in the intimate life and convictions of the people which are more instinctive than opinions. . . . A study of

those changes - a revelation and diagnosis of the hidden life of England - would be a study exceedingly worth attempting to-day. It would be a study which, passing from the external organisation, the condition of trade, the variation in fortune, would endeavour to tear out the inner secret of the life of this people: to exhibit the temper, mettle, response, character of an island race at a particular period of its supremacy. (8)

Just as the novels of the 1840s are often regarded as a response to Carlyle's admonition to take a hard look at 'the Condition of England', and that they do so 'from within', so *Howards End* might well be considered a response to Masterman's plea for a diagnosis of the 'hidden life', the 'inner secret' (his phrases are apposite in the context of 'fiction as history') of 'Liberal England'.

The 'condition of England' during the fourteen years before the Great War can only be presented, in the space available, impressionistically. But it is possible, perhaps, to reconstruct an ambience which would at least be recognisable to men like Forster and Masterman.

On 22nd January 1901, Lady Battersea wrote in her diary: 'The emptiness of the great city without the feeling of the Queen's living presence in her Empire, and the sensation of universal change haunted me more than any other sensations'.[3] The proximity of the old Queen's death to the beginning of the new century seemed to have symbolic significance: Victorianism was done with, the 20th century had dawned, change - for good or ill - was the order of the day. Nevertheless, as Leonard Woolf, a Bloomsbury friend of Forster's, wrote in retrospect: 'the main difference in the world before 1914 from the world after 1914 was in the sense of security and the growing belief that it was a supremely good thing for people to be communally and individually happy.'[4] Change and security: Masterman brings the two poles together when he remarks: 'of all illusions of the opening twentieth century perhaps the most remarkable is that of security.' (*COE*. 288) And indeed these two paradoxically coexistent forces are the keynotes of the entire period - 'universal change' and 'the illusion of security'. It is as though Edwardian and Georgian England was suffering from accelerating schizophrenia.

At the top level of its 'split mind', the period was imbued with what T. E. Hulme at the time identified as a debilitating and Romantic '*satisfaction*' with life. Romanticism, says Hulme, is 'spilt religion' - 'because if you don't believe in Heaven, so you begin to believe in a heaven on earth'; and 'Progress' (which is the product of 'satisfaction' or 'security') 'is the modern substitute for religion'. Significantly he sees such attitudes as the product of the decadence of liberal-humanism - 'that flat and insipid optimism which . . . has finally culminated in the state of slush in which we have the misfortune to live.'[5] Hulme, of course, propagating the 'new Classicism' and self-consciously, iconoclastically, 'modern', is himself a manifestation of the other contemporary tendency - the drive for change. Nevertheless, his concept of 'satisfaction' is useful short-hand for the acceptance of permanence, leavened by a kind of social Darwinism, which forms one level of the pre-war 'mind'. The second level is characterised by the restlessness of the period, the desire for change, for purpose, for excitement; by the reaction against the dead weight of the Victorian past; by the propensity for 'revolt', which receives expression in diverse forms and which becomes increasingly and violently importunate as the end of the period approaches. By March 1914, for one member of the old order at least, 'change' had become the bogeyman: Charles Ricketts notes in his journal 'some sort of decivilizing change, latent about us, which expresses itself especially in uncouth sabotage, Suffragette and Post-Impressionism, Cubist and Futurist tendencies.' And related in tone to 'all this post-impressionism in modern life', were 'equally uncouth retrograde tendencies towards stupid pieties and reactionary ideas, Nationalism, etc.' He concludes:

> The fact is, the world at this moment is probably too comfortable and *bored with its liberty* - liberty for what? . . . The common man is finding out the common man's limitations, that is the trouble; the rest is bad temper, hate and total thoughtlessness; hence the passion for movement and change at all costs, a sort of music-hall-turn sense of life.[6]

Despite Ricketts' own 'bad temper' and prejudice, the range and synthesis of his jeremiad is significant: the suffrage movement, modern art, nationalism and a dissatisfied 'common man' are all related by the same forces of hatred, boredom and the demand for change. And indeed, what George Dangerfield calls 'the unconscious rejection of an established security'[7] is common to widely different movements in the period; and it does signify the incipient demise of 'Liberal England'. One thing is certain: in August 1914, five months after Ricketts wrote, the 'decivilizing change latent about us' became very active indeed.

Both levels of the pre-war 'mind' contributed to a mood which found explosive expression in the Great War. 'Satisfaction', a hangover from the late-Victorian past, and deeply self-deceptive in its refusal to recognise or come to terms with the pressures of modern life, could envisage neither the possibility nor the nature of a 20th century war; and it went on declaring that God was in his Heaven even when he was manifestly slipping out of it. 'Restlessness' - a largely undefined intuition about the nature of life in the 20th century - helped to exacerbate the atmosphere of the years up to the war by engendering violent impulses, and finally informed that response to war which saw it as a heroic release from stagnation, boredom and ignominy: the 'escape from eventlessness'.[8] Violence, although often in an unrealised or abstract form, is a persistent feature of Edwardian and Georgian society. Something of this duality of the pre-war 'mind', and of its effects, is captured by H. G. Wells, during the war, in *Mr. Britling Sees It Through* (1916). Mr. Britling is speaking 'before' the outbreak of war:

> People may be too safe. You see we live at the end of a series of secure generations in which none of the great things in life have changed materially. We've grown up with no sense of danger - that is to say with no sense of responsibility. None of us ... ever really believe that life can change very fundamentally anymore for ever. ... And it's just because we are all convinced that we are so safe against a general breakdown that we are able to be so recklessly violent in our special cases.[9]

In that final sentence, Wells neatly summarises the equivocal attitudes of the period.

One important instance of the collision of these forces is the experience of Liberalism itself in the period. Despite Trevor Wilson's argument that the demise of the Liberal Party occurs during, not before, the Great War,[10] Liberalism as a political creed, and equally many of the 'liberal' principles of English parliamentary democracy, were under assault between 1900 and 1914. The intransigence and the extra-parliamentary militancy of the Conservatives, the Ulster Unionists, the Trades Unions and the Suffragettes, all suggest that the values and attitudes enshrined in the power-structures of the later 19th century, were unable to contain the insistent demands of certain increasingly powerful and disaffected groups. Liberalism, with its benevolent but slow-moving reforms, its belief in the inevitability of progress, its paternalistic regard for the working classes, its anti-Imperialist, pacifist tendencies, its firm belief in *laisser-faire* and compromise, and its solid Gladstonian, prosperous, middle-class 'good sense', was becoming increasingly out of touch with the urgent realities of its world. George Dangerfield has aptly identified the 'spirit of whimsy' as characteristic of Liberalism at this time[11] - a fundamental inability to understand the seriousness of the problems it had to deal with. Something of this spirit is apparent in the tone of a letter from Edward Marsh (private secretary to the Home Secretary, Winston Churchill, and editor of *Georgian Poetry*) to Rupert Brooke in September 1911, when the Agadir crisis and several strikes were at their height:

> What a year we are having! . . . I am so glad [the Constitution Bill crisis] happened just when it did, so that the fun wasn't wasted - for the next week it was all entirely forgotten and swallowed up in the strike. One day Sir Edward Grey said to Winston, 'What a remarkable year this has been - the Coronation - the great heat - the strikes - and now the foreign situation' - 'Why', said Winston, 'you've forgotten the Parliament Bill' - and so he had - and so had everybody. . . . But everything sinks into nothing compared with the great question - will there or will there not be a war?[12]

Both the nonchalant 'anxiety' about serious issues and the 'thrill' mentality are symptomatic of the period. It is perhaps significant, in this context, that violence pervades the atmosphere in which liberalism is confronted (most obviously perhaps by the Suffragettes); and that, even more significantly, a pacifist, democratic, liberal government itself comes to employ violence to defeat those hostile to its value system, (Bachelor's Walk, forcible feeding, the use of troops to break strikes, the shooting of three strikers at Tonypandy.) It is a sign, in fact, of the weakness of the liberal position: as Harold Laski has pointed out, the economic base of liberalism was profit-making and property: 'That was the seminal truth that liberalism was never able to see. It did not realize that the political democracy it brought into being was established on the unstated assumption that it would leave untouched the private ownership of the means of production.' Furthermore, as time went on, it became so habituated to its own political forms that it saw them as 'natural'. Those who controlled the system, therefore, assumed 'that an assault upon the privileges by which they lived was, in fact, to attack the basis of civilization'. In defence of the traditional and seemingly 'natural' conception of society, they employed violence, 'and when ideas fly to arms there is no room in society for liberal doctrine.'[13] Laski is not describing the English situation before the war in particular, but he might well have been doing so.

An even more ironic manifestation of the liberal paradox is the case of foreign relations. Traditionally opposed to the stockpiling of armaments, to European treaty-making and to war, it is Liberalism again which finds itself taking part in all these activities, and implicitly approving what seems to have been the common European philosophy of the period: To Ensure Peace, Prepare for War. Army reforms, military conversations, the Anglo-Russian Convention, the building of Dreadnoughts, Lloyd-George's Mansion House speech, Agadir, all indicate the confusion and uncertainty of Liberalism in the context of *realpolitik*. Faced with the internal collapse of Austria-Hungary and Russia, with German imperialism and paranoia about the 'Triple Entente', with press-campaigns at home for more battleships, and with public feeling regarding Germany as 'the enemy' waiting implacably for 'der Tag', Liberal policy was at sixes and sevens. Indeed, as Nicholas Mansergh has put it, the 'impenetrable penumbra of uncertainty' which surrounded England's intentions just before the war helped to make war more certain,[14] and it further reveals the failure of Liberalism to test traditional principles against actual circumstances. This, and current illusions about what sort of a war might be fought, are important aspects of what Masterman, in the passage quoted earlier, saw as 'an unwillingness to face reality'. But then the history of Liberalism in the period is of a failure to recognise the 'signs of the times', or if it does dimly apprehend them to digest their significance.

But the dual tendencies of the time - a sense of security and the drive towards violent change - inform the broad social and cultural life of the nation as a whole. The wealthy upper classes, 'the Conquerors' as Masterman calls them, not only lead a life of excessive opulence, ease and irresponsibility (as innumerable memoirs, biographies and novels make clear), but also reveal, beneath the fine old patina of 'sweet and carefree' pre-war England, unease, a frenetic urge, and a sense of 'things breaking up'. This is especially apparent amongst the intelligent young, who oscillate between the frenzied pursuit of novelty and the obsessive pursuit of worthwhile 'causes'. Michael Fane, the hero of Compton Mackenzie's contemporary novel *Sinister Street* (1913 -14), will act as the representative image of this tendency. At the other end of the social scale, are 'the Multitude' and 'the Prisoners' (Masterman's terms), the poor and the very poor, badly-paid, badly-housed and badly-educated. This class, according to Masterman, is irrevocably bound on the machine of trade and industry, and is passively acceptant of its lot. It comes increasingly under the influence of the sensational press, full of scraps of knowledge, competitive sport, mistrust of 'the foreigner', spy-stories, murder stories, prize-giving competitions, records broken, and barometer-like discussions about the likelihood of war. At another level, of course, which Masterman largely and significantly ignores, the working classes were increasingly mobilised in the trade unions; and, as the period went on, directly confronted the government and the possessing classes.

But the dominant class, and the dominant culture, were both middle-class, as Forster, writing in 1920, was significantly aware:

I had better let the cat out of the bag at once and record my opinion that the character of the English is essentially middle-class. There is a sound historical reason for this, for, since the end of the eighteenth century, the middle classes have been the dominant force in our community. They gained wealth by the Industrial Revolution, political power by the Reform Bill of 1832; they are connected with the rise and organization of the British Empire; they are responsible for the literature of the nineteenth century.... (*AH*.3)

As *Howards End* also focusses on the various levels of the middle-class petit-bourgeois, John Bull and liberal intelligentsia - it seems appropriate to consider them a little more fully. Middle-class life, its culture and values, dominate our image of the period. Above all one thinks of the development of suburbia, especially around London, soaking up the big battalions of clerks and 'new technocrats' that the demands of the age were producing. Masterman devotes an entire chapter to 'the Suburbans', describing them as 'those enormous suburban peoples which are practically the product of the past half-century, and have so greatly increased, even within the last decade'; they cover 'the hills along the northern and southern boundaries of the city, and [spread] their conquests over the quiet fields beyond'. (*COE*.69-70) The early volumes of Henry Williamson's long autobiographical novel, *A Chronicle of Ancient Sunlight*, vividly suggest the quality of life, for a middle-middle-class family during the period from the 1880s to 1914, living in the South-Eastern suburbs of London as they spread down into Kent; and Masterman's account bears them out. The impression one receives is that 'the suburban' lived a respectable, conforming life, was bored by his employment, conditioned by the popular press, had a narrow social life, was exhausted in spirit by mundane stresses, was snobbish, patriotic, xenophobiac, imperialist and royalist, was apathetic towards social reform and politics, poverty-stricken in religious belief, envious and emulatory of the class above it, and either perpetually fearful of slipping back into the class below it or too comfortable to care how the other half lived. At the extreme edges of this massive block exist, on the one hand, the lower middle class, the Kippses, Mr. Pollys and Mr. Lewishams of H. G. Wells' novels, and on the other, the *haute bourgeoisie* of Galsworthy's acid attack on Edwardian complacency, passionlessness and philistinism, *The Island Pharisees* (1909).

The cultural expression of this class, extensive and diverse, offers an excellent guide to the 'inner history' of the period. There are three broad divisions we can make in it: the indigenous culture of the big battalions of the middle class; the work of the liberal intelligentsia, often critical of the former; and the developments of the 'revolutionary' modernist movements in the last few years before the war.

Gertrude Stein's remark that 'there will be a Renaissance of Ruritania whenever the world of reality is being rather more unheroic than usual' is aptly applied to much Edwardian and Georgian art. In painting many late-Victorian tendencies filtered down: the moralism of Watts, the debased Pre-Raphaelitism of

Burne-Jones and Millais, the anecdotalism of Orchardson, the 'Classical-Revivalism' of Leighton and Alma-Tadema (the Chantrey Bequest purchase for the Tate Gallery in 1909 was one of Tadema's pictures). Equally, the New English Art Club, rebellious in the 1880s, was now itself almost a part of the establishment. Indeed the popular giants of Edwardian and Georgian painting were Frank Brangwyn and John Sargent, both associated with the N.E.A.C. Brangwyn's brightly-coloured glorifications of the 'heroic' past offered an exotic escape from the colourlessness of modern existence, and his enormous murals, of eclectic inspiration, suggest both the Edwardian regard for size and splendour as a prerequisite of 'major' painting and the 'satisfaction' of the age. His heroic idealisation of men at work, and the surrounding symbolism of laden trees and rising suns - so hackneyed and grotesquely false in industrial Edwardian England - are the product of a sentimental and unrealistic materialism. But Sargent's portrait-painting of what Osbert Sitwell called 'The Rich Man's Banquet',[15] is part of the iconography of the Edwardian age. His superb technical facility, his eye for superficial characteristics of personality, his ability to give an aura of opulence and class to his sitters, his acceptance of the materialistic values of his age, his power of representing conscientiously the dresses, diamonds, cravats, fur coats and furniture of the wealthy, his ability to gloss and refine, to flatter and beautify the *arrivée*, and his brilliantly 'daring' impressionistic style, all recommended him to the Edwardians. He would have been the portraitist of the Wilcoxes in *Howards End*. Forster's own comments on Sargent's portraits in the bitter essay 'Me, Them and You' (1925) are apposite here:

a pall of upholstery hung over the exhibition. The portraits dominated. Gazing at each other over our heads, they said, 'What would the country do without us? We have got the decorations and the pearls, we make fashions and wars, we have the largest houses and eat the best food, and control the most important industries, and breed the most valuable children, and ours is the Kingdom and the Power and the Glory'. (*AH*.28-9)

The principal characteristic, indeed, of most popular art in the period was that it confirmed complacency and did not disturb; pretty, restful, dexterous, polished, it was the perfect anodyne.

Its nature is inversely defined by an art critic in *The Studio* for August 1911, who bitterly criticised the opposing, 'modern' tendency, 'not altogether wholesome, to insist upon and exalt the ugly and the commonplace, and to choose the bold facts of modern existence as subjects for study.'[16] One thing is certain: he was not looking at the work of the Sargents of his world.

Literature evinces similar tendencies. The poetry that was mostly read by the middle classes was that of later Victorian 'bards' like William Watson and Alfred Austin, the poet laureate, trotting out 'ideas' about Duty, Manhood, Patriotism, Nature, Love and Death in polished, dead orotundities; or it was the patriotic and 'physical force' poetry of men like Kipling, Henley, Newbolt and Noyes. This, of course, is the literary counterpart of popular painting, as a contemporary criticism by Charles Sorley suggests: 'The voice of our poets and men of letters is finely trained and sweet to hear; it teems with sharp saws and rich sentiment; it is a marvel of delicate technique: it pleases, it flatters, it charms, it soothes: it is a living lie'.[17] Even the less hidebound poetry of writers like Chesterton, Housman, de la Mare and Masefield is imbued with a sense of unreality, of fantasy, or of fantasy masquerading as 'realism'. But poetry - until the 'poetry boom' of 1911 and after - was not unduly popular. Arnold Bennett, in a furious contemporary attack on the middle class's 'gigantic temperamental dullness', suggests why this was so: 'only sheer ennui drives [it] to seek distraction in the artist's work. It prefers the novelists among artists because the novel gives the longest surcease from boredom'.[18] Thus, in H. G. Wells' novel, *Ann Veronica* (1909), the heroine's father 'read but little, and that chiefly healthy light fiction with chromatic titles, *The Red Sword*, *The Black Helmet*, *The Purple Robe*, in order to "distract his mind" '.[19] It was novelists like E. F. Benson, Robert Hichens, Marie Corelli, Hall Caine, Elinor Glyn and Mrs. Humphrey Ward, who in their different ways supplied the Edwardian readers' needs, readers who, wrote Masterman, 'seek romance - and find it - in a complex murder-case, in stories of crime . . . in stories dependent in their appeal upon sudden vicissitudes of fortune in which chance or resolution are always breaking down the insupportable sequences of cause and effect.' (*COE*.262) And in words which tend to generalise the incidence of the attitudes expressed by the *Studio* art critic above, he says: ' "escape" is the prominent aspect of to-day's art, in a deliberate turning-away from the realities of the present, which only a few accept as substance for artistic interpretation'. (232) Perhaps it is significant that the outstandingly popular stage-play of the period should have been J. M. Barrie's *Peter Pan*, which epitomises the escape-wish.

It is not surprising that this situation produced a response from the writers of the so-called 'Liberal Revival'. Shaw, Galsworthy - in novels and plays - Conrad, Bennett, Wells, the young D. H. Lawrence, Forster himself, all expose and pillory the materialism, soullessness and complacency of the 'philistines'. These writers may be regarded as a part of that radical-liberal tradition which E. J. Hobsbawm identifies as the only significant body of thought attacking the ethos of imperialism and finance capitalism in England before the war.[20] Two points, however, should be made: firstly, they express a growing disenchantment as writers because, as Masterman noted, they make 'no impression upon the contented, boisterous spirit of Middle Class England' (*COE*.261); they begin, in other words, to register the liberal intellectual's sense of alienation from the mass of readers. And secondly, although their attack is intelligent and accurate, it does not lead them beyond their own prevailing world-view. Like Masterman, they may *sense* cataclysmic change to be imminent, but they do not *conceive* of it.

If writers like these identify, at least mildly, the 'rejection of established security', and a revolt against the 'satisfaction' of popular culture, the new art movements of the period from 1910 to 1914 establish it very clearly. Charles Ricketts' attack on 'all this Post-Impressionism in modern life' suggests how modern movements were related, in certain sections of the contemporary mind, with other forms of social disaffection, and that they heralded 'decivilising change'. But for those who were sympathetic, too, 'Post-Impressionism' represented a radically new order of being. For Virginia Woolf, at least, it was of massive significance; she remarked that 'on or about 31st December 1910, the human character changed',[21] and she had in mind the impact of the first of Roger Fry's Post-Impressionist exhibitions at the Grafton Galleries. In a general public sense the exhibition was a *succès d'exécration* (*The Times* of late 1910 saw it as witnessing the rejection of 'all that civilization had done',) but it opened the way, over the next four years, for an explosion of experimentation in the arts in England - and particularly amongst those artists and writers who had the 'classical' theories of T. E. Hulme in common: Ezra Pound and the Imagists, Wyndham Lewis and the Vorticists. Despite some fine creative achievements, both movements were essentially propagandist in nature, self-consciously 'revolutionary'. Their activity was, as Lewis said later, 'Art behaving as if it were politics', his group's main aim being 'to hustle the cultural Britannia'.[22] 'We are the Primitive Mercenaries of the Modern World', claimed one of the manifestoes in *B L A S T* (1914), the 'puce-coloured monster' which was the mouthpiece of Vorticism and, to some extent, of Pound as well. 'To make the rich of the community shed their education skin, to destroy politeness, standardisation and academic, that is civilized, vision, is the task we have set ourselves.' And significantly, *B L A S T* acclaimed the Suffragettes: 'We admire your Energy.' Hulme and Pound expressed similar attitudes; around 1909, Hulme announced: 'Personally I am of course in favour of the complete destruction of all verse more than twenty years old'.[23] And in a letter of 1913, Pound wrote that the new poetry would cause

> a *Howl*. They won't like it. It's absolutely the *last* obsequies of the Victorian period. . . . It's not futurism and it's not post-impressionism, but it's work contemporary with these schools. . . . I guarantee you *one* thing. The reader will not be *bored*. He will say ahg, ahg, ahg, ahhh, but - bu - bu - but this isn't poetry.[24]

The propaganda, the formal experimentation, and, amongst the painters more particularly, an interest in violence, reveal the dynamic 'recklessness' and drive for change which we have noticed is the undertone of the whole period, and which is particularly and increasingly distinct in the intellectual revolt. Around 1904 in Cambridge, Leonard Woolf remembered, there was 'a conscious revolt against the social, political, religious, moral, intellectual, and artistic institutions, beliefs and standards of our fathers and grandfathers'; by 1911, he adds, it was even more insistent.[25] But for all this recklessness 'in our special cases', to borrow Wells' phrase, there was no real sense of a world coming to an end: that is a post-war perception. A *sense* of change - for good or evil - there may have been, but the violent upheaval that was coming remained a sense only, and could be easily dismissed, as 'senses' can. Wyndham Lewis, writing retrospectively of his own violent 'special case', Vorticism, in fact speaks for the whole period:

'Kill John Bull with Art!' I shouted. And John and Mrs. Bull leapt for joy in a cynical convulsion. For they felt as safe as houses. So did I.[26]

Such movements and tendencies are symptoms of the changing world in which *Howards End* was written; a world, not then but later, revealed to be increasingly inimical to the values the novel enshrines. But there is, finally, one movement, 'Georgianism', which although part of the ferment of the last four or five years before the war, is more indigenously characteristic of 'Liberal England' than any other. And *Howards End* might well be regarded as a 'Georgian' novel.

Georgianism was self-consciously a part of the 'revolt' of the period, and yet we can see it now as the final gentle expression of the 19th century English romantic tradition. It seemed modern, but it was of the past. The 'modernist' poets, predictably, abhorred it; and the Great War not only destroyed many of its poets, but effectively revealed its inadequacies as a modern poetic idiom. The first *Georgian Poetry* anthology (1912)[27] - there was never strictly a 'school' with a defined poetic - was the brainchild of Edward Marsh, and its composition was very largely defined by Marsh's admiration for the work of Rupert Brooke. The poetry, for the most part, was a gentle, uncomplicated lyricism, written in the accents of common speech and celebrating common things. Apart from some passages of rather immature 'brutality' (in Brooke's poems especially) there is little which confronts the harsh realities of modern existence. Equally, it is most *un*revolutionary in form, ('I wonder where you find the Post-Impressionism,' Marsh wrote in 1913 in reply to Robert Bridges, 'I thought I had kept out all that sort of thing.[28]) Many of the poems rely on impressions and simple emotional responses, which tends to encourage a self-indulgent 'satisfaction' with things (pleasant things) as they are. Brooke's 'Dining Room Tea' is the apotheosis of these qualities, and indeed, it could be regarded as the representative poem of 'Georgian England' - or perhaps its epitaph:

... The laughter played
Unbroken round me; and the jest
Flashed on. And we that knew the best
Down wonderful hours grew happier yet.
I sang at heart, and talked, and eat,

And lived from laugh to laugh, I too,

When you were there, and you, and you.

But the most pervasive feature of Georgian poetry is what may be termed 'pure patriotism' - the celebration of 'rural England'. Many of the poems are simply reportage of particular aspects of the countryside and its passing culture, others more subtly idealise their subject and create what F. R. Leavis has called 'poetical realities'[29] - images whose existence is totally defined and circumscribed by their own poetic terms. In particular, 'England' becomes a place of refuge from England: the poetic eye is invariably *off* the harsh intruding reality of, for example, urban life and *on* the vision of a static rural paradise. W.H. Davies in 'The Mind's Liberty', for instance, 'dissolves' his subject - which is ostensibly Charing Cross - by writing that even amid its feverish activity, 'I oft-times hear sweet Malpas Brook, /That flows thrice fifty miles away'. And John Drinkwater, in 'A Town Window', transmutes 'a drab inglorious street' by noting that '. . . the frost and clean starlight/ As over Warwick woods are sweet.' More explicitly, Brooke's 'The Old Vicarage; Grantchester' sincerely idealises the English countryside:

Ah God! to see the branches stir

Across the moon at Grantchester . . .

and for a significant purpose: Brooke longs for

Deep meadows yet, for to forget

The lies, and truths, and pain.

Whatever self-mockery was intended, the poem's residual emotion is one of nostalgia for an idealised Cambridgeshire. In 'Georgian England' such responses were still possible - even for a young intellectual who was a member of the Cambridge 'Carbonari', gripped by atheism and socialism. Something of this optimism, and this reverence for 'rural England', informs *Howards End*, too. But Forster had a stronger sense of the insecurity of his values, and his novel expresses this, although it does not finally *admit* it. Only the war would reveal the truth of his fears. Of his pre-war existence, Forster later wrote:

We were full of hopes then, easily-held hopes, we did not know the severity of the problems which Fate was reserving for us. (*TC*.237)

FORSTER AND THE LIBERAL DILEMMA

In one of Forster's few poems, 'A Voter's Dilemma' (1923), he refers to 'The word that's graven on my heart/*Nineteen Fourteen*' (*AH*.31); and in 'The Consolations of History' (1920), he writes:

> As a general rule, anything that ends abruptly must be given bad marks; for instance, the fourth century B. C. at Athens, the year 1492 in Italy, and the summer of 1914 everywhere. (*AH*.165)

There is a fair amount of irony in this sentence, but the basic truth of it remains - for Forster and for the majority of his contemporaries. August 1914, certainly in retrospect and probably at the time, was like a door shut in the face. Whatever premonitions there may have been, they were now faced with facts. Forster's vision was darkened and the 'hopes' of the period of *Howards End* were gone. Towards the end of 'A Voter's Dilemma', Forster writes of

> The way of blood and fire and tears
>
> And pestilence and profiteers -
>
> The way that mankind has been
>
> Since nineteen hundred and fourteen.

For Forster, the world had gone wrong after 1914, as many of his essays in the twenties, thirties and forties indicate. There are constant references - often in essays ostensibly about something else - to what Pound's Mauberley calls a 'botched civilization': at the end of an obituary note about Roger Fry, there is an image of him moving 'down the sinister corridor of our age', (*AH*.41); in 'The Consolations of History', a reference to 'existence as it threatens today - a draggled mass of elderly people and barbed wire', (*AH*.164); a passing comment, in 'Bishop Judd's Book', that the volume's binding 'recently cracked, like much else in my time', (*TC*.192); a reference in an essay on Gide and Stefan George to 'this age of misery' (*TC*.234); a reference in 'In My Library' to 'the days before the world broke up', (*TC*.305); and so on and so on. Such comments represent the ground-bass of much of Forster's thinking after the war. There is nothing published which suggests that Forster thought like this *before* the war. Of course he attacked the materialism and philistinism of the English middle class - indeed this is the central theme of all the short stories and novels up to 1914 (including the posthumously-published *Maurice*) - but he was attacking what he was later to describe as 'the undeveloped heart' (*AH*.5), rather than fighting a rearguard action against vast forces of 'decivilization'. In any case, there was always the possibility then, that individual hearts could be 'developed', and society saved by those who had 'the passion' rather than 'the prose' in their souls. *Howards End*, as we shall see, demonstrates this, at one of its levels.

The point I wish to make is that there is no 'liberal crisis' before the Great War for Forster or for most other liberal-humanists: at least at the conscious or conceptual level. That is a phenomenon of the inter-war period and beyond. It was *then*, for men like Forster, the crisis for 'civilized' values became of intense conscious concern. Of course the crisis is foretold in the world before 1914, as I have attempted to make clear in the previous section: in the pressure for change; in the political failures of Liberalism; in the size and nature of the power-blocs and their armaments; in the accelerating development of urban conurbations, of the motor car, of the cinema, of aeroplanes, of mass-production techniques; in the social disaffection, class hostility, sex hostility; in the violent rejection of the Victorian past, its aims and ideals; in the increasing dominance of the popular press; in the writers' growing alienation from a 'philistine', 'half-educated', public; in the radical reassessment of the role and nature of art by the 'classical' anti-humanism of Hulme and other modernists; in the fears, occasionally expressed (by Conrad, for instance, in *Heart of Darkness* (1902) - this is a largely 'pre-Freudian' world, we should remember) that under the thin crust of civilization lay barbaric, primitive forces only just held in check; even in the social criticism of the radical-liberal intellectuals themselves. Masterman, once again, sensed the uncertainty of things:

with the vertical division between nation and nation armed to the teeth, and the horizontal division between rich and poor which has become a cosmopolitan fissure, the future of progress is still doubtful and precarious. (*COE*.303)

But against all these factors was set a certain optimism, a belief in the efficacy of the 'old verities', a sense of fundamental stability even if the forms of things changed, of being able to achieve one's aims *within* the existing structures of civilization. To put it over crudely perhaps, there was the belief that while 'society' could and should be reformed, 'civilization' was an eternal principle. And that is the ideological 'fault' that the war revealed.

Liberalism, as Harold Laski has pointed out, 'was, effectively, a by-product of the effort of the middle class to win its place in the sun' and its economic base is capitalism, profit-making and the acquisition of property. Liberalism is, therefore, an *ideology* — 'one more particular of history seeking to masquerade as a universal'. Its fundamental function, at the political level, was 'to serve the owners of property', but as time went on it became so obsessed with the quality of the political forms and of the civilization it had created, 'that it failed adequately to take into account [its] dependence upon the economic foundation they expressed'.[1] This is the crux of the liberal crisis: liberals forgot liberalism was an ideology and believed that it and civilization were synonymous. Only in this century have liberals fully comprehended their error, and none more acutely than sincere proponents of liberal-humanist values like Forster.

Liberal-humanist 'values' (at the moral and cultural levels, rather than the actively political) are the product of middle-class culture in the ascendancy, and especially of that culture's élite. They assume the gradual improvement of the quality of life for the whole people through reform and education, but *within* the existing social and economic structure and in the image of the culture of the élite. The fundamental articles of faith are the sanctity of the individual and the ideal development, therefore, of 'the culture of the whole man'. From these principles all the other values spring and also the liberal dilemma. Tolerance, liberty, reason, generosity, freedom of speech, democracy, non-aggression, reform of public abuses, respect for civil rights, personal relations, civilized discourse, the regard for art, the intellect and tradition: all these represent the values of liberal-humanism. They are expressed as well as anywhere in Matthew Arnold's writings on culture, and in the famous phrase 'sweetness and light':

> Culture, which is the study of perfection, leads us . . . to conceive of true human perfection as a *harmonious* perfection, developing all sides of our humanity; and as a *general* perfection, developing all parts of our society. . . . Culture has one great passion, the passion for sweetness and light. It has one even yet greater! - the passion for making them *prevail*. It is not satisfied till we *all* come to a perfect man; it knows that the sweetness and light of the few must be imperfect until the raw and unkindled masses of humanity are touched with sweetness and light.[2]

These are fine values but what do they rest on, and do they involve 'all parts of our society'? They rest, of course, on exploitation and hence on ascendancy; and that rests on having wealth, or, putting it another way, on the *possibility* of leading a life in which the cultivation of such values is viable. And this is where the problem lies: only some individuals can achieve the culture of 'the whole man', the majority remain in a material and spiritual outer darkness. Forster himself recognised this: 'The hungry and the homeless don't care about liberty any more than they care about cultural heritage. To pretend that they do care is cant.' (*AH*.63) Educating those without the material base to support the values of liberal civilization is futile; and yet how does one offer everyone the opportunity for 'culture' without destroying precisely that material base which makes possible all the values one wishes to propagate? Doesn't the civilization of liberal-humanism - even at its most brilliant or benevolent - *necessarily* rest on the fact that other people produce goods and remove the garbage? This is the crux of the problem, and it is not an entirely post-war perception, for the economic base of liberal civilization had been increasingly recognised in the later decades of the 19th century. Nevertheless it remained possible for radical-liberal thought to believe in the efficacy of humanist values, especially in the 'development' of the individual as the prerequisite of communal improvement. What *is* characteristic of the post-war situation, is the assault on liberal civilization manifested in vast depersonalised forces: total war, totalitarian systems, mass movements, mass production, mass communications. Such forces, more or less consciously, disregard liberal-humanist civilization, and the liberal-humanist is forced to defend his values. But the defence is undermined by a consciousness of the dilemmas outlined above: that the 'values' rest on money, injustice and inequality. Thus he sees all his values, good in themselves, under threat of destruction but he can neither offer a consistent defence of his position, nor join one of the forces which seem to be in the process of smashing all he most reveres. He stands, therefore, observing 'barbarism' victorious, able only to affirm the value of his values as a despairing gesture in a situation where, as Raymond Williams put it, 'failure and breakdown [are] common and inevitable'. (See above p.13). His only dignified posture is that of someone like Forster who will give 'two cheers' for values he passionately believes in, while recognising that these values are doomed to destruction by the new culture he sees about him and knows to be inferior. 'This hideous dilemma,' Forster vividly evokes in 'Post-Munich' (1939): Liberal-humanists recognise 'that if Fascism wins we are done for, and that we must become Fascists to win'. If they could 'sell themselves' to one side or another, they might find peace, but

they are too fine to sell themselves: that is their glory and their trouble. They see through all the slogans. Their grasp on reality paralyses them. Paradoxically, they become more and more negative and ineffective, until leadership passes to their inferiors. (*TC*.34)

Forster, indeed, is himself one of the clearest and most conscious spokesmen of the crisis of the liberal conscience this century, and his essays in *Abinger Harvest* and *Two Cheers for Democracy* offer a running definition of the dilemma. Perhaps the classic statement of it is in 'The Challenge of Our Time' (1946):

I belong to the fag-end of Victorian liberalism, and can look back to an age whose challenges were moderate in their tone, and the cloud on whose horizon was no bigger than a man's hand. In many ways it was an admirable age. It practised benevolence and philanthropy, was humane and intellectually curious, upheld free speech, had little colour-prejudice, believed that individuals are and should be different, and entertained a

41

sincere faith in the progress of society. The world was to become better and better, chiefly through the spread of parliamentary institutions. The education I received in those far-off and fantastic days made me soft and I am very glad it did, for I have seen plenty of hardness since, and I know it does not even pay. Think of the end of Mussolini - the hard man, hanging upside-down like a turkey, with his dead mistress swinging beside him. But though the education was humane it was imperfect, inasmuch as we none of us realized our economic position. In came the nice fat dividends, up rose the lofty thoughts, and we did not realize that all the time we were exploiting the poor of our own country and the backward races abroad, and getting bigger profits from our investments than we should. We refused to face this unpalatable truth. . . .

All that has changed in the present century. The dividends have shrunk to decent proportions and have in some cases disappeared. The poor have kicked. The backward races are kicking - and more power to their boots. Which means that life has become less comfortable for the Victorian liberal, and that our outlook, which seems to me admirable, has lost the basis of golden sovereigns upon which it originally rose, and now hangs over the abyss. . . .

If we are to answer the Challenge of our Time successfully, we must manage to combine the new economy and the old morality. The doctrine of *laissez-faire* will not work in the material world. It has led to the black market and the capitalist jungle. We must have planning and ration books and controls, or millions of people will have nowhere to live and nothing to eat. On the other hand, the doctrine of *laissez-faire* is the only one that seems to work in the world of the spirit; if you plan and control men's minds you stunt them, you get the censorship, the secret police, the road to serfdom, the community of slaves. (*TC*.65-6)

This is a highly revealing passage in a number of ways. It suggests many of the values of which Forster's liberal-humanism is composed and it relates them explicitly to the Victorian/liberal tradition. It also confirms our sense of the pre-war past - especially the Edwardian/Georgian trust in progress - and establishes Forster's attitudes as endemic to it. And it reveals the liberal

42

dilemma. Firstly, there is the ambivalence about Forster's pre-war education which is both 'admirable' and 'inadequate'. Secondly it emphasises the money-base of liberal civilization and the recognition of this 'unpalatable truth' *only after* the war when the 'dividends' were already disappearing. Thirdly, there is Forster's paradoxical awareness that the exploited peoples' 'kicking', radically threatens the liberal outlook (which is nevertheless admirable). Fourthly, it reveals Forster's unwillingness, even now, to comprehend the real relationship between economic base and cultural superstructure in his desperate attempt to reconcile the 'new economy' and the 'old morality'. Finally, in the imagery of the last paragraph, there is a tacit acceptance that the landscape of the present is dominated by forces inimical to 'culture'.

Forster's values, then, belong to the liberal-humanist tradition of the 19th and early 20th centuries. They are essentially part of that long critical response to industrialism and materialism which the Victorian intelligentsia developed, and which receives its most 'Forsterian' form in Matthew Arnold's work - 'of all the Victorians most to my taste'. (*TC*.201) Both see ancient Greece as a model civilization, both believe in the central importance of 'Culture', both had 'doubts' although, as Forster recognises, 'Matthew Arnold's "bad days" are Halcyon when compared with our own', Arnold only faintly heard 'the collapse of all civilization, so realistic for us'. (*AH*.71) Both, too, were primarily critics of 'materialism', 'philistinism', 'barbarism', 'the undeveloped heart', and saw these as the products of industrialisation and finance capitalism. A society controlled by such forces, both believed, is inimical to the best values of liberal-humanism, especially individual liberty, personal relations and the development of a healthy common 'culture'. (The central irony of the liberal position is again apparent: the head rejects its own body.) Hence their mutual regard for the Past, Tradition and 'the Land'. Something of Forster's regard for the pre-industrial past is expressed in his sympathetic essay, 'Mrs. Hannah More' (1928; in *AH*.), and in his essay on Ferney, Voltaire's country house:

Lucky, happy we, to get this last peep at one of the symbols of European civilization. Civilization. Humanity. Enjoyment. That was what the agreeable white building said to us, that was what we carried away. It was not a large building and that has been part of the disaster. It was too small to cope with the modern world. A Ferney today would have to be enormous, with rolling staircases and microphones, if it was to function proportionately, and if it was enormous could it be Ferney? (*TC*.344-5)

But for Forster, writing in the middle decades of the 20th century, there are vestiges of 'civilization' left even in that 19th century which Arnold had admonished - but then Arnold had not experienced 'the collapse of all civilization'. Thus despite Forster's satire, in the pre-war novels and stories, on 'Victorian' materialism and philistinism, he realises after the war that his values belong to that past:

> Those of us who were brought up in the old order, when Fate advanced slowly, and tragedies were manageable, and human dignity possible, know that that order has vanished from the earth. We are not so foolish as to suppose that fragments of it can be salvaged on some desert island. But since it is the best thing we knew or are capable of knowing, it has become a habit which no facts can alter. (*TC*.40)

This state of mind accounts for his gentle and nostalgic treatment of Victorian middle-class life in essays like 'Battersea Rise' (1934; in *AH.*) or 'Henry Thornton' (1939), in which modern 'values' are critically juxtaposed with those of even the most solidly respectable past:

> Family Prayers went out with the family. When the children were limited and the servants went into factories and the death-duties cut property to pieces, these daily gatherings of piety and plenty came to a natural end. Little houses have been built today upon the noble lawns of Battersea Rise, and upon the site of its great library which William Pitt designed, and those little houses listen to the religious service on the wireless, if they listen at all. (*TC*.198)

The pre-war past is for the older Forster very much the swan-song of liberal-humanist civilization. It is not insignificant, perhaps, that another liberal 'critic' of the pre-war period, John Galsworthy, should begin *The Forsyte Saga* as an attack on Victorian materialism, and then go on, in the volumes published after the war, to idealise what he had previously mocked - the 'old' civilization. Perhaps the comparison is unfair to Forster, but it reveals something of that paradox of Edwardian/Georgian England: 'I only kill the thing I love.'

Forster's regard for the past relates, of course, to his love for 'rural England' and the old houses which represent its culture - liberal-humanism as a whole way of life. It is noticeable that Margaret in *Howards End* should think to herself, while looking at the Hertfordshire countryside, 'Left to itself . . . this county would vote Liberal'. (249-50) Liberal culture is most fully expressed in the civilization of rural England, but this, as we know, is threatened by the forces of 'London', representing depersonalised *largeness*. (Notice in the passage on Ferney, above, how the house 'was too small to cope with the modern world'; Howards End, too, is 'old and *little* and altogether delightful'. (*HE*.5)) This means, of course, that liberal culture as a whole is threatened; and significantly, one of the ways in which Forster expresses his horror and fear of modern civilization is through the destructiveness of the 'planners' and of the encroaching towns. In a famous passage from 'The Challenge of Our Time', he describes the end of a rural community he knew and loved well; 'the whole area' has been commandeered by the planners for a new town of 60,000 people:

> The people now living and working there are doomed; it is death in life for them and they move in a nightmare. . . . the satellite town has finished them off as completely as it will obliterate the ancient and delicate scenery. . . .
>
> 'Well', says the voice of planning and progress, 'why this sentimentality? People must have houses.' They must, and I think of working-class friends in north London who have to bring up four children in two rooms, and many are even worse off than that. But I cannot equate the problem. It is a collision of loyalties. I cannot free myself from the conviction that something irreplaceable has been destroyed, and that a little piece of England has died as surely as if a bomb had hit it. I wonder what compensation there is in the world of the spirit, for the destruction of the life here, the life of tradition. (*TC*.67-8)

Once again one recognises the liberal conflict. In the struggle between individual and community, the liberal wishes to support the former *in the interests* of the community, but finds himself, in fact, opposed to the community. It will be worth remembering this passage when we discuss *Howards End*, since the novel is prescient of the same dangers to traditional culture. But the difference between the pre- and post-war position is that while Forster now resignedly watches the planners victorious, in *Howards End* 'rural England' is made to triumph.

After 'the world broke up', the values enshrined for Forster in what had been 'Liberal England', were Dodos in an alien world. Nevertheless, their intrinsic worth remained, and Forster, like so many other liberal-humanists, attempted to live by and affirm them, *while recognising their impotence*. That is the true 'liberal tragedy' of the 20th century - perhaps most brutally exposed in the 1930s - and it has by no means been resolved yet. Forster's own clearest statement of it is in the address he gave to the *Congrès International des Ecrivains* at Paris on 21st June 1935:

> My colleagues . . . may feel that it is waste of time to talk about freedom and tradition when the economic structure of society is unsatisfactory. They may say that if there is another war writers of the individualistic and liberalizing type, like myself and Mr. Aldous Huxley, will be swept away. I am sure that we shall be swept away, and I think furthermore that there may be another war. It seems to me that if nations keep on amassing armaments, they can no more help discharging their filth than an animal which keeps on eating can stop itself from excreting. This being so, my job, and the job of those who feel with me, is an interim job. We have just to go on tinkering as well as we can with our old tools until the crash comes When the crash comes, nothing is any good. After it - if there is an after - the task of civilization will be carried on by people whose training has been different from my own.
>
> I am worried by thoughts of a war oftener than by thoughts of my own death, yet the line to be adopted over both these nuisances is the same. One must behave as if one is immortal, and as if civilization is eternal. Both statements are false - I shall not survive, no more will the great globe itself - both of them must be assumed to be true if we are to go on eating and working and travelling, and keep open a few breathing holes for the human spirit. (*AH*.67)

It is a moving passage, not least in its brutal acceptance of the failure of the 'life of values'.

What, then, for Forster himself were these values that he could not forego? The fundamental principle of his liberal-humanism was a passionate regard for the individual. In 'The Challenge of Our Time', he writes:

> I have no mystic faith in the people. I have in the individual. He seems to me a divine achievement and I mistrust any view which belittles him. . . . When there is a collision of principles would you favour the individual at the expense of the community as I would? Or would you prefer economic justice for all at the expense of personal freedom? (*TC*.66-7)

Derived from this position, of course, is his famous comment in 'What I Believe' (1939): 'if I had to choose between betraying my country and betraying my friend, I hope I should have the guts to betray my country'. (*TC*.76) He continues: 'Love and loyalty to an individual can run counter to the claims of the State. When they do - down with the State, say I, which means that the State would down me'. Despite the despairing realism of this final perception, it is apparent that Forster's individualism is not derived, at the most basic level, from political doctrine. Its inception lies, rather, in a deeply personal, almost mystical, conception of 'Life'. He believes in what he calls 'the unseen', a sort of spiritual 'life-force', not entirely dissimilar to that of D. H. Lawrence, although less robustly defined. Forster himself uses vague terms to express it, as for example in the list of nouns he presents while explaining the absence of 'the unseen' in Henry Thornton: 'Poetry, mystery, passion, ecstasy, music.' (*TC*.199) Elsewhere, in an attempt to describe it, he borrows Keats' phrase, 'the Holiness of the Heart's Affections'. (*TC*.82) In the early stories it is represented by a figure like Pan, a spirit opposed to the deadening materialism of middle-class existence. Perhaps the closest one can come to defining it is to say that it is 'the life of the spirit' informing the entire being of an individual, the fully 'developed heart' realising all a man's potential for life. It is what Arnold meant by 'culture'.

Such a belief was reinforced by Forster's reading of G. E. Moore's *Principia Ethica* (1903), a philosophical treatise which influenced many of Forster's generation in the early years of the century, and in particular those of the Cambridge and

'Bloomsbury' circles. Moore's principal tenets are that the best kind of life would be achieved by the pursuit of Love and Beauty and that these are realised most fully in personal relations and in Art. 'Personal relations' is a concept at the centre of the individualism expounded in 'What I Believe', and implies a regard for love, tolerance, liberty and the full development of what, in *Howards End*, Forster calls the inner life, the life of passion and poetry. Equally, the importance of Art is a constant theme in his essays, representing as it does a civilized bulwark against the depredations of barbarism. Its inner order and harmony are healing in a chaotic world, because it is the tangible proof of the human spirit's supremacy over the destructive element:

> No violence can destroy it, no sneering can belittle it. Based on an integrity in man's nature which lies deeper than moral integrity, it rises to heights of triumph which give us cause to hope. (*TC*.230)

Forster's liberal-humanism and the nature and role of art converge in this context, and will lead us on, in the next section, to some discussion of the novel form and Forster's relationship to it. Here, let me add one final, related, twist to the liberal dilemma. One of the central problems for liberal individualism has been (and was in the 19th century) the engendering of 'developed hearts', the education of very large numbers of people into the 'whole' culture of liberal civilization. How, in Arnold's words, to make 'sweetness and light *prevail*'? How, to put it more crudely, to make a *private* good a public force? This of course raises the whole question of the liberal state's economic base but it also poses the problem of the relationship between liberal culture and society. The culture of the individual is essentially a self-fulfilling private activity, and this very individualism contributes to the sense of crisis: liberal culture regarding itself as an organic and beneficial social force, remains isolated in the midst of the society it wishes to educate and serve. 'Love' and 'personal relations' are, in effect, private and individualising (witness Forster's remarks about betraying his country rather than his friend); and Forster recognises this. In the essay on 'Tolerance' (1941), he rejects 'Love' as the 'spiritual quality needed to rebuild civilization', and proposes the 'dull virtue' of tolerance instead:

> Love is a great force in private life; it is indeed the greatest of all things; but love in public affairs does not work . . . The fact is we can only love what we know personally. And we cannot know much. (*TC*.54)

He identifies the dilemma even more clearly in 'What I Believe'. Writing of 'the experiment of early life', he says it is not a failure -

> but it may well be hailed as a tragedy, the tragedy being that no device has been found by which these private decencies can be transmitted to public affairs. (*TC*.82)

It is worth noting here, perhaps, that the Schlegel sisters in *Howards End* also 'desired that public life should mirror whatever is good in the life within'. (*HE*.28)

Precisely this problem has lain at the centre of the realistic novel's treatment of society and the individual from its very beginning, although it becomes more insistent in the 19th century. Both Dickens and George Eliot, for example, in very different ways, are confronted by the problem of how the 'good heart' or the 'morally mature' nature can have public resonance. The novelists may create individuals who have achieved full maturity, but how does this improve society as a whole, how is this *publicly* realised? The question is never really answered. Dickens, increasingly less certain, *hopes* that the 'good heart' will triumph, but he does not explore the process; George Eliot proposes the gradual accretion of morally significant actions and characters as the way forward, but their public impact is never concretely realized in the texture of the novels. Even in *Daniel Deronda*, where a public role is designed for Daniel, it is actually expressed in visionary terms for the future. For Forster, as we have heard, 'Art' is the expression of man's highest state of being, and it is in art that 'vision' can be realized, indeed that is a crucial feature of its importance. In a signficant passage in 'What I Believe', Forster discusses the problem of 'force and violence' *vis à vis* 'civilization', and posits the value of art as visionary affirmation:

> I believe that [force] exists, and that one of our jobs is to prevent it from getting out of its box. It gets out sooner or later, and then it destroys us and all the lovely things which we have made. But it is not out all the time, for the fortunate reason that the strong are so stupid. Consider their conduct for a

moment in the Niebelung's Ring. The giants there have the guns, or in other words the gold; but they do nothing with it, they do not realize that they are all-powerful, with the result that the catastrophe is delayed and the castle of Walhalla, insecure but glorious, fronts the storms. . . . The Valkyries are symbols not only of courage but of intelligence; they represent the human spirit snatching its opportunity while the going is good, and one of them even finds time to love. Brünnhilde's last song hymns the recurrence of love, and since it is the privilege of art to exaggerate, she goes even further, and proclaims the love which is eternally triumphant and feeds upon freedom, and lives.

So that is what I feel about force and violence. It is, alas! the ultimate reality on this earth, but it does not always get to the front. Some people call its absences 'decadence'; I call them 'civilization' and find in such interludes the chief justification for the human experiment. (*TC*.78-9)

Forster's use of a programmatised Wagner here is significant in two ways: firstly, as an example of what he sees as the affirmatory function of art, 'exaggerating' the eternal triumph of love; secondly because Forster uses a similar device in *Howards End* - Helen's interpretation of Beethoven's Fifth Symphony. Such a strategy is noteworthy here because this is a novel which itself employs Art to affirm a vision - that of 'Liberal England' triumphant. Private values are there allowed public efficacy.

4

FORSTER AND THE NOVEL

Forster is not foursquare in the English realistic tradition. Despite his devotion to Jane Austen, his admiration for *Moll Flanders* and his regard for George Eliot and Thackeray, he reveals other interests in *Aspects of the Novel* and those of his essays which deal with fiction. He writes sympathetically about Virginia Woolf, Proust, Ronald Firbank, Sterne, Forrest Reid, Dostoevsky, Hardy, D. H. Lawrence, Melville, Gide, Samuel Butler; an oddly-assorted collection of novelists, but all of whom, in fact, employ non-realistic or 'fictional' modes for expression. Of Samuel Butler's *Erewhon*, Forster writes in a significant essay entitled 'A Book that Influenced Me' (1944), '*Erewhon* also influenced me in its technique. I like that idea of fantasy, of muddling up the actual and the impossible until the reader isn't sure which is which, and I have sometimes tried to do it when writing myself'. (*TC.*266) Forster's inclinations are certainly towards modes of expression which involve 'fantastic', 'visionary' or 'poetic' formulations, as some light-hearted remarks in 'George Crabbe and Peter Grimes' (1948) suggest:

> It amuses me to think what an opera on Peter Grimes would have been like if I had written it. I should certainly have starred the murdered apprentices. I should have introduced their ghosts in the last scene, rising out of the estuary, on either side of the vengeful greybeard, blood and fire would have been thrown in the tenor's face, hell would have opened, and on a mixture of *Don Juan* and the *Freischütz* I should have lowered my final curtain. (*TC.*190)

And his own fictional practice adumbrates this interest in 'non-realism'.

In defining Forster's relationship to the 'crisis' of realism in the 20th century, we must be careful not to overemphasize and distort. Nevertheless there is a problem of mode in *Howards End* which is related to the ideology the novel contains, and Forster is not alone amongst 20th century novelists in discovering it. After all the novel form itself is a product of the liberal-humanist world view, and when the latter begins to disintegrate, there is bound to be a problem of fictional expression. Yet it would be quite absurd to argue that Forster moves *towards* a 'non-realistic' form, since, if anything, he is more concerned with a realistic texture in *Howards End* than he was in the 'fantasies' and the more obviously fabular earlier novels. The paradox is, rather, that Forster clearly wishes to come to terms with the 'phenomenal world', but the only way he can do so, *within* the liberal-humanist ideology and as the 20th century gains momentum, is by employing 'contrived' modes of expression which wrench it into step with his vision.

For Forster fiction is an ambivalent zone, 'bounded by two chains of mountains neither of which rises very abruptly - the opposing ranges of Poetry and of History - and bounded on the third side by a sea', which is 'prophecy' or 'vision'. (*AN*.14) It is a 'mixed art' (*TC*.127), combining elements of 'Poetry' and of 'the life of facts'. (*AH*.146) Nevertheless if a novel is a work of art, it will be 'a self-contained entity, with a life of its own imposed on it by the creator. It has internal order'. (*TC*.97) Forster's argument is that the various elements must be balanced *within* the book so that it is 'convincing' but not, of course, 'real'. Of literary works in general, Forster writes:

> It is their power to create not only atmosphere, but a world, which, while it lasts, seems more real and solid than this daily existence of pickpockets and tramps. . . . We [enter] a universe that only answers to its own laws, supports itself, internally coheres, and has a new standard of truth. Information is true if it is accurate. A poem is true if it hangs together. . . . It is not this world, its laws are not the laws of science or logic, its conclusions not those of common sense. And it causes us to suspend our ordinary judgments. (*TC*.89-90)

Much of what Forster says here is very true of the strange alchemy of literary form; the novelist at his best, for instance, will indulge in 'faking' and persuade us to accept improbabilities. But we must be wary of the argument which places all literary works *beyond* 'ordinary judgments', especially if the works *purport* to be 'real' and to be concerned with 'this world'. And if the 'faking' is obtrusive (i.e. is not 'internally coherent' and 'convincing') one may well question the validity of the 'new standard of truth'.

Interestingly enough, Forster includes two somewhat idiosyncratic components of 'the novel', 'Fantasy' and 'Prophecy', among the conventional factors ('story', 'plot', 'people') he discusses in *Aspects of the Novel*. Certain books, he says, contain these elements which make them difficult to assess by ordinary criteria. Neither quality is very clearly defined in his book, but they are certainly connected with 'the unseen', the 'life of the spirit', which we have noticed lies at the root of Forster's beliefs. They are described as 'a beam of light' which intensifies and illuminates, but whose connection with the rest of the book's texture is intangible. And again there is an element of special pleading in his discussion of them:

> What does fantasy ask of us? It asks us to pay something extra. It compels us to an adjustment that is different to an adjustment required by a work of art, to an additional adjustment. The other novelists say 'Here is something that might occur in your lives,' the fantasist 'Here is something that could not occur. I must ask you first to accept my book as a whole, and secondly to accept certain things in my book.' (113-4)

And of the novelist of 'Prophecy', he writes:

> we shall neglect as far as we can the problems of common sense. As far as we can: for all novels contain tables and chairs, and most readers of fiction look for them first. Before we condemn him for affectation and distortion we must realize his viewpoint. He is not looking at the tables and chairs at all, and that is why they are out of focus. We only see what he does not focus - not what he does - and in our blindness we laugh at him. (130)

What the special pleading reveals, however, is Forster's awareness of the need for techniques which are beyond realism. Elsewhere he remarks how little 'innovation in form' (*AH*.111-2) there has been in the English novel between Fielding and Arnold Bennett. And it is for this reason that he writes sympathetically about Proust, Gide, Virginia Woolf and even Gertrude Stein (for her futile attempt to break the 'life in time' structure of novels. (*AN*.48-9)) Some of his most self-revealing comments, in fact, occur in the two essays he wrote on Virginia Woolf whose attitudes to life and art are so similar to his own. He constantly picks out for comment her uneasy use of realism, compared with her assured 'poetic' manner. In the 1941 essay he criticises *Night and Day*:

> This is an exercise in classical realism, and contains all that has characterized English fiction, for good and evil, during the last two hundred years: faith in personal relations, recourse to humorous side-shows, geographical exactitude, insistence on petty social differences: indeed most of the devices she so gaily derides in *Mr Bennett and Mrs Brown*. The style has been normalized and dulled. (*TC*.253)

And in the 1925 essay, at the end of an almost identical passage, he had added: 'Surely the writer is using tools that don't belong to her.' (*AH*.106) Again, in the later essay, he identifies the dilemma of 'poetry' and 'realism' even more clearly:

> And this is her great difficulty. Holding on with one hand to poetry, she stretches and stretches to grasp things which are best gained by letting go of poetry. She would not let go, and I think she was quite right, though critics who like a novel to be a novel will disagree. (*TC*.257)

Forster's acute perception of Virginia Woolf's 'difficulty' here, may be read an an oblique commentary on his own problems. And it is ironically significant that in her brilliant essay 'The Novels of E. M. Forster', Virginia Woolf should identify in his work precisely the same 'difficulty'; of *The Longest Journey*, she writes:

> The contrast between poetry and realism is much more precipitous. . . . His old maids, his clergy, are the most lifelike we have had since Jane Austen laid down the pen. But he has into the bargain what Jane Austen had not - the impulses of a poet. . . . Here, then, is a difficult family of gifts to persuade to live in harmony together: satire and sympathy; fantasy and fact; poetry and a prim moral sense. No wonder that we are often aware of contrary currents that run counter to each other. . . . (*CE*.I.344)

The accuracy of Virginia Woolf's final judgment here applies equally well to *Howards End*. She also refers, however, to the 'one slim volume . . . that he has allowed himself of pure fantasy', the short stories, which represent 'an attempt on Mr. Forster's part to *simplify the problem which so often troubles him of connecting the prose and poetry of life*'. (347. My italics.) But she recognises that it is not a mode he could remain in for long, and that indeed he returns to the complex world of *Howards End*. It is a significant perception. What she does not go on to say, however, is that even in *Howards End*, as we shall see later, a type of 'fantasy' is used to 'simplify' precisely the same 'problem'.

Certainly Forster's early stories celebrate the 'poetry' of life in a form which is unequivocally 'fantastic', and the novels before *Howards End* are overtly fabular too. Despite the devastating social satire on the Edwardian suburban world, their primary aim is to affirm the 'life of the spirit' at a predominantly mystical level. This is most obviously apparent in the use of the 'spirit of Italy' as a regenerative force in *Where Angels Fear to Tread* and *A Room with a View*, and in the heavily symbolic use of Stephen Wonham, 'Wiltshire' and the Cadbury Rings in *The Longest Journey*. The fabular quality of these works is intensified by Forster's definite and systematic patterning of character, plot, texture and symbolism. All three novels are consciously *artificial* and they make a statement *about* life in allegoric terms. Their 'vision' is moral and spiritual, rather than pragmatic and social, and the 'life of facts', the satire, the 'old maids, and clergy', are merely supports for the moral theme. In this sense, the novels work exclusively within their own terms of reference, 'answering to their own laws', and concerned with a 'truth' which is quite valid within the prescribed realm of the informing 'vision'. In *Howards End*, however, Forster is much more concerned with a *social* vision, and as a result the 'life of facts' (with the consequent realism of treatment) becomes more insistent. But this the 'vision' finds difficult to accommodate, and Forster has to employ fictional contrivance to achieve resolution. The 'realistic' and 'contrived' modes tend to repel each other, and strains begin to show. It is at this point of formal dissolution that the novel, as we shall see below, proffers historical significance at the 'unintentional' level.

It is *Maurice*, however, and some of Forster's comments on it, which are most revealing in the context of realism's limitations.

Written next after *Howards End*, between 1913 and 1914, (it was partly revised later, and not published until after Forster's death), *Maurice* continues to explore the concerns and problems of *Howards End - before* the Great War broke out. Forster wrote, in a letter to Forrest Reid: ' "I was trying to connect up and use all the fragments I was born with" - well you had it exhaustingly in *Howards End*, and Maurice, though his fragments are more scanty and bizarre than Margaret's, is working at the same job . . .'[1] And despite the fact that Maurice is made to be something of a 'Wilcox' as well as a 'Schlegel', and that the novel is concerned with homosexual love, the concern with the triumph of the inner life is the same. But because the 'expression' of this concern is in terms of homosexuality, which was considerably more taboo before the Great War than it is now, there is a much stronger sense in the book of *withdrawal* from the world: not through escapist 'fantasy' but because of the *isolation* (a recurrent word in *Maurice*) of the homosexual. This, in turn, affects the form of the book.

Forster is concerned to render the world from the homosexual point of view which thus precludes a presentation of the 'normal', i.e. heterosexually-perceived, world of most realistic fiction. In short and pointed chapters, and in a style which is direct and functional, he presents an 'impression' of this acentric view, as though sloughing off, paradoxically, the 'pretence' of realism in his urgency to present the experience. This is apparent, too, in his continuous use of dreams and trance-like states of mind to express himself; and we may note Forster's own comment on Maurice's adolescence: 'Where all is obscure and unrealized the best similitude is a dream. Maurice had two dreams at school; they will interpret him'. (*M*.25) This sentence exactly expresses both Forster's direct, 'non-realistic', manner of address in the novel, and his conscious reliance on 'fabulous' modes in a situation where the 'normal' world has fragmented *Maurice*, at such times, is indeed close to 'fabulation'. And elsewhere, the novel confirms Forster's uncertain relationship with realism: in the extensive use of iterative motifs and symbols; in the closely patterned texture; and, as his 'Terminal Note' makes clear, in the carefully constructed representative characters. (*M*.218-20).

Finally, Forster's comments on the 'happy ending', with which he had much trouble, reveal how deeply committed he was to the idea of 'Art' as the medium in which 'vision' could be realised, indeed could often *only* be realised. (See above pp 45-50) In this particular case, of course, Forster wishes to assert the possibility of permanent happiness for a homosexual relationship, *even though* the 'facts' of English society are solidly against it. One might notice, too, that if homosexual love here expresses the 'inner life', then Forster's presentation of its victory is even more implicitly problematic than it is at the end of *Howards End*. In a letter to Lowes Dickinson in December 1914, he wrote 'but the temptation's overwhelming to grant to one's creations a happiness actual life does not supply. "Why not?" I kept thinking. "A little rearrangement, rather better luck - but no doubt the rearrangement's fundamental. It's the yearning for permanence that leads a novelist into theories towards the end of each book'.[2] Such a remark applies equally well to the ending of *Howards End*. Later, even more explicitly, he explains that fiction, far from being 'realistic', is a way of realising situations which would be impossible in real life: 'A happy ending was imperative. . . . I was determined that in fiction anyway two men should fall in love and remain in it for the ever and ever that fiction allows, and in this sense Maurice and Alec still roam the greenwood. I dedicated it "To a Happier Year" and not altogether vainly.' (*M.* 218). Further on in the same piece, however, he implicitly admits the irony of that 'happier year'; the novel has 'dated', he says, 'because it belongs to an England where it was still possible to get lost. It belongs to the last moment of the greenwood. *The Longest Journey* belongs there too, and has similarities of atmosphere. Our greenwood ended catastrophically and inevitably'. (221) One might add that *Howards End*, with its 'happy ending . . . that fiction allows', belongs there too; although its more ambiguous vision and texture comprehend the 'end of the greenwood' more completely. But *Maurice* remains fascinating evidence of Forster's recognition that conventional realism was limited when an 'abnormal' world was to be defined, or when an ideal vision demanded realisation.

But as with the 'crisis' of liberalism, the problem for the novelist was more harshly defined in the post-war world and Forster himself does not solve it. His only further novel is *A Passage to India* (1922), and in this, where he recognises the impotence of his values against the obliterating echo of the Marabar

Caves, he makes no attempt to reconcile the 'visionary' and the 'mundane'. Those characters who achieve peace through vision accept it as something other-worldly, and Forster himself does not impose Hindu passivity and 'acceptance' as a solution to social and cultural disharmony. Nor is there a final, resolved, 'connection' between Europe and India here. In this sense, *A Passage to India consciously* expresses the revealed crisis of the liberal-humanist position and of the liberal-realist novel: in a world where the 'connections' of the one are effete, so too is the kind of fiction which embodied them. Forster wrote no more novels.

It is illuminating in this context to consider Forster in relation to Hardy, who stopped writing novels almost as Forster began. And we might notice first, Forster's significantly expressed admiration for Hardy in *Aspects of the Novel*: 'Meredith did know what the novel could stand . . . [but] the work of Hardy is my home and that of Meredith cannot be'. (*AN*.101-2) The implication is that Hardy, happily, did *not* know what the novel 'could stand', and indeed it is in his bending and forcing of its structures that much of his importance lies. Forster clearly sympathises with this; but there are interesting similarities in their work too. Both novelists have a profound, almost mystical, response to the English countryside and its living embodiment of the past; both novelists perceive it to be in the process of radical and destructive change; both novelists write books which tend to be 'representative' of a condition of being; both rely heavily on myth and symbolism, on passages of poetic intensification, on coincidence, chance and contingency; both approach melodrama; and yet both still, to an extent, attempt to work within the conventions of the realistic novel. This is not the place for an extended interpretation of Hardy, nor indeed for an extended comparison with Forster, but it is worth noticing in passing how characters, objects and action in their novels are continuously *imbued* (they do not merely assume it) with connotative significance. Where Hardy 'sacrifices' Tess at Stonehenge, with all its symbolic penumbra, Forster brings Rickie, in *The Longest Journey*, up against the living past at the Cadbury Rings; where Forster uses Sawston to express a whole inhuman society, Hardy uses Christminster in *Jude*; where the threshing machine in *Tess* embodies a radical social reorientation, so does the motor-car in *Howards End*;

where Leonard Bast is 'smothered' by books, Clym Yeobright is 'blinded' by self-education; where Alec, and all he represents, is destructively 'connected' to Tess, Henry Wilcox is to Leonard and Jackie Bast; where Arabella and Sue (the flesh and the spirit) battle over Jude, Agnes and Ansell struggle over Rickie, and so on. This is not to say that the 'significance', or indeed the effect, of these random examples, is the same, but to suggest that the *approach* is similar. And to add, that such symbolic action is generally presented *as though it were* matter of fact. Thus Hardy's need to express Tess's heredity (the pressure of the past in her present) has to be realised in such strangely 'actual' scenes as that where Angel Clare, while sleep-walking, deposits her in a stone coffin (Chapter XXXVII). And Forster, to keep alive the prophetic sense of Margaret's rightful 'inheritance' of Howards End, has to employ the 'mistakes' of the dotty retainer, Miss Avery. Both novelists, in other words, work in a mixed mode, from which springs much of the continuing interest, much of the tension and ambiguity, of their work.

Both Hardy and Forster are writers whose world-view was fragmenting: 'the ache of modernism' and 'panic and emptiness', 'the blighted star' and 'the goblin footfall', are symptomatic of the same insecurity, of a world which they thought they knew disintegrating and being differently re-formed before their eyes. Describing 'things as they really are' becomes increasingly impossible when the sense of change and breakdown is too insistent, and finding a mode to express *a sense* of 'our race . . . . . degenerating' (*HE*.149), or 'the coming universal wish not to live',[3] *within* the conventions of the realistic novel form, poses a real problem. To express either a vision of the dissolution of the past and the present, or a vision of the ideal future, requires something other than the apparatus of verisimilitude. Sterne had made his point about the futility of systems - literary or epistemological - in the expressive form of *Tristram Shandy*; the Gothic novelists had accommodated their neuroses in fantasy; Dickens had encapsulated his deepening sense of human evil in the grotesque. But in general the English novelists had accepted that they could 'see life steadily and see it whole', and had written within that brief. Literary realism has meant an acceptance that, in Henry James's phrase, the 'splendid waste' of real life has some palpable existence, and that prose fiction purports to be closely referential to it: that verisimilitude is both possible and needful. When a novelist feels that this acceptance is eroded, then the referential mode is irrelevant. Hardy, it seems to me, was searching for a new structure in which to embody his vision of disintegration but he remained at least partly hamstrung by the tradition of verisimilitude (Little Father Time, in *Jude*, is the most obvious example of this ambivalence), hence the heterogeneous modes of his novels, his refusal to write more fiction after *Jude the Obscure*, and his attempt at another epic medium in *The Dynasts*. Forster's remarks about Hardy, in the section on 'Plot' in *Aspects of the Novel*, suggest something of the sympathetic understanding he had for Hardy's work:

> Hardy seems to me essentially a poet, who conceives of his novels from an enormous height. They are to be tragedies or tragi-comedies, they are to give out the sound of hammer-strokes as they proceed; in other words, Hardy arranges events with emphasis on causality, the ground plan is a plot, and the characters are ordered to acquiesce in its requirements. Except in the person of Tess (who conveys the feeling that she is greater than destiny), this aspect of his work is unsatisfactory. . . . . . Hardy's success in *The Dynasts* (where he uses another medium) is complete, there the hammer strokes are heard, cause and effect enchain the characters despite their struggles, complete contact between the actors and the plot is established. . . . But in the novels, though the same superb and terrible machine works, it never catches humanity in its teeth. (*AN*.100-1)

Much of this, especially the dominance of causality and the coercive power of the plot, is, as we shall see, true for Forster too. The nature of the vision, however, is very different. Until after the war and *A Passage to India*, Forster seems to be avoiding the creation of constructs of despair; in *Howards End*, at least, he attempts to affirm a system of values against the destructive forces. Perhaps it is Hardy's unwillingness to legislate, his readiness only to locate and enact, in complex images, a state of being at a point of radical change, which makes him the greater novelist. For instance, 'the President of the Immortals', Tess's 'heredity', the inescapable contingency of her relationship with Alec, the letter to Angel under the carpet, their honeymoon house, Angel's response to her confession, her experiences at Flintcomb Ash, and so on, are all *metaphors,* in *Tess of the D'Urbervilles,* for Tess's victimisation by the allied pressures of a society in the throes of profound change. She is trapped by the age, and indeed becomes an image of one aspect of its consciousness, as Jude more completely does in the later novel. Hardy is not saying this must or must not happen, nor is he saying that a metaphysical 'Fate' rules the universe, and he is not bemoaning the passing of a way of life. He is merely attempting to give form to his consciousness of the impalpable processes of cultural change. Where Hardy's use of causality is merely an objective correlative for affairs he wishes to express, Forster's is a device for getting his own way. Nevertheless, the problem remains much the same: How does one define a vision in terms of the conventions of referential realism? And especially, as in Forster's case, if the implications of the vision are opposed to the logic of the circumambient reality?

Hardy and Forster both stopped writing novels after they had completed their most uncompromising fictional statements. Hardy, it is plausible to consider, stopped writing fiction because he had taken it beyond its own limits as he saw them; and he chose another medium, which, as we saw above, Forster significantly admired. His vision could no longer be expressed in the novel form. And Forster, too, seems to have considered the novel played out as far as he was concerned. *A Passage to India* is the final fictional expression of his vision - and the vision has become bleak, private, exclusive, realised only within. (It is not without point that this, Forster's last novel, is set outside, and is not 'about', England.) Having no public 'transmission', how can it be defined, especially in the novel form whose great quality, Forster himself recognises, is its 'humanity', its concern with 'the immense richness of material that life provides'? (*AN*.164) A vision which has social resonance can be given form, even if uncertainly in a novel like *Howards End*; but a vision which is socially unrealisable cannot be given 'realistic' definition. That is the impasse.

But this is partly explained by the nature of 'visionary' writers anyway. In an essay on Forrest Reid (and it is interesting that Forster should have admired this not widely-read, mystical writer so much), he makes some interesting remarks about them:

Vision is only one of the instruments that the imagination provides and those artists who select it develop on different lines from their empirical brethren. They do not, like Shakespeare or Goethe, pick up something and then something more. Everything comes to them in a rush, their arms are filled at once with material for a life's work, and their task to sort and re-sort what they have rather than to seek fresh experiences. (*AH*.79)

In other words, for the visionary writer, the 'idea' is pre-eminent, not 'the immense richness of material that life provides' And Forster himself is not unlike this, (although as Virginia Woolf perceived, he is part 'realist' too.) He has a vision when he begins to write and finds social formulations to express it - more realistically, and so less securely, by the time he is writing *Howards End*. Then comes the war; the vision is radically affected, and affected in a way which proscribes its social realisation. Forster stops writing novels. He does not seek 'fresh experiences' from ' the immense richness of material that life provides', because it is the vision which is important and not the forms of life. But his vision is now inexpressible. It is here that our two 'crises' intersect and reveal themselves: in an alien world the 'vision' is inorganic, and therefore there can be no referential, 'realistic' expression of it. A retreat into the 'magical island' of fantasy was no longer possible for Forster, nor was the fictional definition of the new reality - that was a task for others. It is significant here to remember Forster's comments, quoted earlier, about the major modern writers: 'These writers look outside them and find their material lying about in the world. But they arrange it and re-create it within, temporarily sheltered from the pitiless blasts and the fog'. (*TC*.284) However, for Forster between 1908 and 1910, most things were still possible, even though the weather was worsening.

HOWARDS END: FICTION AS HISTORY

> Looking back on the past six months, Margaret realized the chaotic nature of our daily life, and its difference from the orderly sequence that has been fabricated by historians. (*HE*.101)

So Maragret Schlegel muses, with Forster behind her. And the sentence leads us back to our concern with the novel as history, reminiscent as it is of Carlyle's description, quoted earlier, of life as 'a Chaos of Being' rather than the 'linear narrative' that History makes it. And *Howards End* - a novel about the middle classes and their attitudes to life in late Edwardian England - attempts to realise an 'historical' situation as 'solid Action'. That, over-simply, is Forster's conscious contribution to 'history from within'; and the first part of this section will describe what that history is. But the novelist uses 'narrative' too; and he may 'fabricate' an 'orderly sequence' of events which also misrepresents the 'chaotic nature' of life. What does the selection, arrangement and expression of the material reveal to us about the writer's view of 'the past' and of society? What is his ideological standpoint? In our case, of course, the 'historian' is also a novelist, and the novel is our 'source'. Much of our sense of the underlying *stance* of the book, therefore, will derive from its formal ordering and expression. *Howards End*, as 'history from within', enacts both a history of its own time and place in its formal and thematic structures, and is 'prophetic' of situations - literary and social - which were to be fully realised well after it was written.

Howards End is concerned with money and its relationship to the life of liberal-humanist values. At one point, Helen asks Margaret,

> '. . . did you say money is the warp of the world?'
> 'Yes.'
> 'Then what's the woof?'
> 'Very much what one chooses', said Margaret, 'It's something

that isn't money – one can't say more.' (122)

Margaret's 'something' is defined in the course of the book in a number of ways, but suffice it to say for the moment that it is connected with the 'life of the spirit', 'the unseen', the 'life of values'. The novel as a whole is concerned to establish the 'connections' between 'the warp of the world' and 'values'. Earlier, Margaret writes to Helen:

> 'Don't brood too much . . . on the superiority of the unseen to the seen. It's true, but to brood on it is medieval. Our business is not to contrast the two, but to reconcile them.' (98)

As we shall see later, Forster consistently uses Margaret as a mouthpiece for his own attitudes, so here we may assume that he sees it as 'modern', rather than 'medieval', to attempt to reconcile base and superstructure, wealth and culture. Forster's perception of the critical reliance of liberal civilization on factors which it often despises and rejects, is a significant instance of the late 19th and early 20th century recognition of the paradox. And the early 20th century liberal-humanist is concerned to effect the necessary, clear-sighted reconciliation, to 'connect'.

Within the novel, Forster considers the problem in terms of the middle classes alone:

> We are not concerned with the very poor. They are unthinkable, and only to be approached by the statistician or the poet. The story deals with gentlefolk, or with those who are obliged to pretend that they are gentlefolk. (44)

There is a disarming honesty about this dismissal· of 'the very poor'; but if the novel *is* largely concerned with 'the condition of England', it is very revealing of the Liberal dilemma, and we must return to it. The middle classes are represented by three families: the Wilcoxes, wealthy upper-middle class; the Basts, lower-middle-class on the very edge of poverty; the Schlegels, liberal intelligentsia of part-German stock, cultivated, with unearned incomes. *Howards End* at one level is concerned with the 'private' world of these individuals, their relationships and interconnections. But these quite clearly have representative status, and 'history from within' will lie in the 'public' resonance of densely-textured 'private' lives. The nature of the novel's realism, its ability to convince, will therefore be an important consideration in assessing the nature and validity of its 'history'.

The principal 'internal' context for the action of *Howards End* is the conflict between 'London' and 'the Earth' which the passage I discussed earlier suggested, and which is related, of course, to the 'external' contexts defined in Chapters 2 and 3 above. But if Forster's patterning of characters and action is to be understood, it requires slightly fuller description.

> London was but a foretaste of this nomadic civilization which is altering human nature so profoundly, and throws upon personal relations a stress greater than they have ever borne before. Under cosmopolitanism, if it comes, we shall receive no help from the earth. Trees and meadows and mountains will only be a spectacle, and the binding force that they once exercised on character must be entrusted to Love alone. May Love be equal to the task! (243)

For Forster, 'London' clearly represents the dominant tendencies of modern life, restless, always on the move, changing, fragmenting - 'bricks and mortar rising and falling with the restlessness of the water in a fountain, as the city receives more and more men upon her soil'. (45) One of the iterative motifs of the book is of buildings being pulled down to make way for yet vaster buildings. (This, of course, is what happens to the Schlegels' quiet and cultured house in Wickham Place). The character of London is artificial and frenetic: 'Electric lights sizzled and jagged in the main thoroughfares, gas-lamps in the side streets glimmered a canary gold or green. The sky was a crimson battlefield of spring, but London was not afraid. Her smoke mitigated the splendour . . . She had never known the clear-cut armies of the purer air'. (115) These physical characteristics affect the inner lives of its inhabitants - 'London only stimulates, it cannot sustain' (141) - and it smashes their stored and time-warranted culture:

> The Schlegels were certainly the poorer for the loss of Wickham Place. It had helped to balance their lives, and almost to counsel them. Nor is their ground-landlord spiritually the richer. He has built flats on its site, his motor cars grow swifter, his exposures of Socialism more trenchant. But he has spilt the precious distillation of the years, and no chemistry of his can give it back to society again. (141)

London is not only destructive it is also the centre of a spreading contagion. Significantly, the Schlegels' 'ground-landlord' is of the Wilcox race and it is their motor-cars and their exodus to suburbia which spread the destructive tendencies. The Great North Road, which 'should have been bordered all its length with glebe', except that 'Henry's kind had filched most of it' (310), now only offers 'such life as is conferred by the stench of motor-cars, and . . . such culture as is implied by the advertisements of antibilious pills.' (15) Charles Wilcox's motor-car settles dust all over the villages he passes through, and - unconscious of irony - he comments: ' "I wonder when they'll learn wisdom and tar the roads" '. (19) Margaret Schlegel, on the 'unreal' journey to Oniton for Evie's wedding, and with her developing love of 'the land', expresses a different view: 'They had no part with the earth and its emotions. They were dust, and a stink, and cosmopolitan chatter . . .' (200)

'London', and what it is destroying, is clearly related to the principal actors in the drama. Charles Wilcox first has a neat little modern house in Surrey then moves to Hilton, the village which contains 'the station for Howards End': 'being near London, it had not shared in the rural decay, and its long High Street had budded out right and left into residential estates'. (15) In fact, of course, for Forster, Hilton represents one type of 'rural decay'. Margaret, however, 'belongs' to Howards End, which is 'old and little, and altogether delightful' (5): 'she was struck by the fertility of the soil; she had seldom been in a garden where the flowers looked so well, and even the weeds she was idly plucking out of the porch were intensely green'. (187) Of such places, Forster is later to remark - and, in so doing, offer his most explicit definition of what 'England' means to him -

In these English farms, if anywhere, one might see life steadily and see it whole, group in one vision its transitoriness and its eternal youth, connect - connect without bitterness until all men are brothers. (250)

And Howards End itself is clearly symbolic of this culture, as a deleted passage in the manuscript, shortly before this, makes even more explicit.[1] (It is also worth noticing in passing, Forster's use of Matthew Arnold's famous line: 'Who saw life steadily, and saw it whole'.[2] It expresses what 'Culture', in its full Arnoldian sense, means for him and he uses it recurrently in the course of *Howards*

End to define states of cultural being.) But 'these English farms' are threatened. 'Howards End' and 'London' are the two sides in an unequal battle and the battle is in a sense being fought at Hilton. Hilton represents a point of change: it is suburbia, but it is also close to Howards End; past and present are in uneasy juxtaposition here: breaking its rows of 'tiled and slated houses' are 'six Danish tumuli . . . tombs of soldiers'. (15-16) And Forster significantly continues:

> The station, like the scenery, . . . struck an indeterminate note. Into which country will it lead, England or Suburbia? (16)

The distinction Forster makes is a pointed one: 'England' is *not* suburbia, it is, in effect, 'Howards End' and the question he asks at this point of impending change is: Which will be victorious? He puts the question another way at the end of a chapter which has described 'England' from the Purbeck Hills:

> . . . . For what end are her fair complexities, her changes of soil, her sinuous coast? Does she belong to those who have moulded her and made her feared by other lands, or to those who have added nothing to her power, but have somehow seen her, seen the whole island at once, lying as a jewel in a silver sea, sailing as a ship of souls, with all the brave world's fleet accompanying her towards eternity? (165)

Who does England belong to, and who will she belong to in the future? It is a question that Masterman asks at the beginning of *The Condition of England*, and it is the question which *Howards End* poses - and attempts to resolve.

The Wilcoxes are men of property. As finance capitalists they make money and they make money work. Both Henry and Charles (father and elder son) are men of action and decision in the City. They know what they have to do and they do it. Henry 'felt that his hands were on all the ropes of life, and that what he did not know could not be worth knowing'. (124) They work hard and successfully, they buy and sell houses, they drive motor-cars and are pillars of the Edwardian, conservative, middle-class establishment. They dislike cosmopolitan culture, Socialism, women's emancipation, foreigners, and so on. If anything, Charles is more extreme in his Wilcoxism than his father, and it is not insignificant that he regards Helen Schlegel as 'the family foe' (288), because she too represents the logical extreme of the Schlegel attitude to life. Charles is tough, resolute and consistent. Paul, the younger son, is an imperialist with a strongly-developed sense of duty to country and Empire: ' "A nation who can produce men of that sort" ', says Margaret, ' "may well be proud. . . . . . An Empire bores me so far, but I can appreciate the heroism that builds it up" '. (105-6) Between them, then, the Wilcox men represent aspects of Victorian and Edwardian materialism at its most successful. Only Evie, the daughter, who has the forms of this world without its force, lacks their 'conquerors' charm. Significantly, this is a masculine world in which women have a precise and circumscribed place. The Wilcoxes lack the 'feminine' gifts. They are devoid of imagination, passion, sentiment, 'poetry'; they do have affection but they are unable to express it; they have no 'inner life', are unaware of 'the unseen'. They are the type, says Forster pointedly, who 'saw life more steadily, though with the steadiness of the half-closed eye'. (301) They are, indeed, the 'Philistines', the 'Island Pharisees', Masterman's 'Conquerors' whom, he says, 'must not expect much from themselves beyond rulership'. (*COE*.61) They have no regard for the Past, culture or 'personal relations'; and behind the armour-plating which they present to the world is the 'panic and emptiness' which Helen describes when their values will no longer 'pay'. Ostensibly they are the owners or 'inheritors' of England, and they do actually *own* Howards End - although they regard it as ' "picturesque enough, but not a place to live in" '. (128) They have enclosed part of the meadow and attempted to build a garage under the wych-elm. In Forster's terms, then, they cannot be true 'heirs' of England; at one point, as a motor-car passes, he comments:

> In it was another type, whom Nature favours - the Imperial. Healthy, ever in motion, it hopes to inherit the earth. It breeds as quickly as the yeoman, and as soundly; strong is the temptation to acclaim it as a super-yeoman, who carries his country's virtue overseas. But the Imperialist is not what he thinks or seems. He is a destroyer. He prepares the way for cosmopolitanism, and though his ambitions may be fulfilled, the earth that he inherits will be grey. (301)

Nevertheless, part of Forster's liberal 'realism' lies in the recognition, mainly expressed through Margaret Schlegel, of the Wilcoxes' 'place' in the world. They are the 'warp' of life, and 'necessary':

> She desired to protect them, and often felt that they could protect her, excelling where she was deficient. Once past the rocks of emotion, they knew so well what to do, whom to send for; their hands were on all the ropes, they had grit as well as grittiness, and she valued grit enormously. They led a life that she could not attain to - the outer life of 'telegrams and anger'. . . . To Margaret this life was to remain a real force. She could not despise it, as Helen and Tibby affected to do. It fostered such virtues as neatness, decision, and obedience, virtues of the second rank, no doubt, but they have formed our civilization. They form character, too; Margaret could not doubt it: they keep the soul from becoming sloppy. How dare Schlegels despise Wilcoxes, when it takes all sorts to make a world? (98)

And her extraordinary conversation with Miss Avery, a true 'yeoman' of the old type, confirms the ambiguity of their relationship to 'England':

> 'This house lies too much on the land for them. Naturally, they were glad enough to slip in at first. But Wilcoxes are better than nothing, as I see you've found.'
> Margaret laughed.
> 'They keep a place going, don't they? Yes, it is just that.'
> 'They keep England going, it is my opinion.'
> But Miss Avery upset her by replying: 'Ay, they breed like rabbits. Well, well, it's a funny world.' . . .
> 'They breed and they also work,' said Margaret, ... 'It certainly is a funny world, but so long as men like my husband and his sons govern it, I think it'll never be a bad one - never really bad.'
> 'No, better'n nothing,' said Miss Avery, and turned to the wych-elm. (255)

Forster never excuses the Wilcoxes their failings; 'personal relations' and the superiority of the 'inner life' remain the ideal, and we may notice in evidence the way their attitude to Mrs. Wilcox's bequest of Howards End to Margaret is explained but not condoned: 'The practical moralist may acquit them absolutely. He who strives to look deeper may acquit them - almost. For one hard fact remains. They did neglect a personal appeal. The woman who had died did say to them, "Do this", and they answered, "We will not" '. (94) But Forster is pragmatic, too; the 'life of the spirit' is only possible if it is securely based on wealth. Therefore the Wilcoxes are, in part, 'heirs', and they deserve recognition: 'Someday - in the millenium - there may be no need for [this] type. At present, homage is due to it from those who think themselves superior, and who possibly are.' (152)

As proof of the need for wealth to be truly cultured, Forster presents Leonard Bast, a clerk living on the edge of the abyss of poverty, trapped into marriage with Jacky by his own feckless good nature, bored by his work, hating his material conditions, and desperately trying to 'acquire culture' (39) by assiduous study of Ruskin and other Victorian educators: 'Leonard listened to it [Ruskin's 'voice' in *The Stones of Venice*] with reverence. He felt that he was being done good to, and that if he kept on with Ruskin, and the Queen's Hall Concerts, and some pictures by Watts, he would one day push his head out of the grey waters and see the universe. He believed in sudden conversion . . .' (48) A little later, however, he has a more realistic perception, phrased again, significantly, in Matthew Arnold's words; 'To see life steadily and see it whole was not for the likes of him.' (53) Whereas the Wilcoxes are the possessors who make culture possible, even if they do not have it themselves, the Basts illustrate negatively the reliance of the 'culture of the whole man' on material prosperity. Forster makes this explicit after the affair of Leonard's 'stolen' umbrella:

For that little incident had impressed the three women more than might be supposed. It remained as a goblin foot-fall, as a hint that all is not for the best in the best of all possible worlds, and that beneath these superstructures of wealth and art there wanders an ill-fed boy, who has recovered his umbrella indeed, but who has left no address behind him, and no name. (44)

Bast, in fact, is another 'type' of modern English society. He is one of the 'losers', a modern figure and yet connected in the past to the 'England' which London and Wilcoxism are destroying. It is significant that Forster stresses his rural heritage (see below, and *H.E.*221), and that it is Henry Wilcox who effectively 'ruins' both Jacky and Leonard Bast. Forster describes Leonard 'representatively':

a young man, colourless, toneless, who had already the mournful eyes above a drooping moustache that are so common in London, and that haunt some streets of the city like accusing presences. One guessed him as the third generation, grandson to the shepherd or ploughboy whom civilization had sucked into the town; as one of the thousands who have lost the life of the body and failed to reach the life of the spirit. . . . . Margaret . . . wondered whether it paid to give up the glory of the animal for a tail coat and a couple of ideas. Culture had worked in her own case, but during the last few weeks she had doubted whether it humanized the majority, so wide and so widening is the gulf that stretches between the natural and the philosophic man, so many the good chaps who are wrecked in trying to cross it. She knew this type very well - the vague aspirations, the mental dishonesty, the familiarity with the outsides of books. She knew the very tones in which he would address her. (109)

One notices here, again, the questioning of the efficacy of 'Culture', the difficulties inherent in Matthew Arnold's proposal that 'sweetness and light' should *prevail*. Nevertheless, despite Bast's unattractiveness and hopelessness, Forster's complex vision of the constituent threads in the fabric of middle-class England, recognises a quality in him which redeems his life: he has 'the spirit of adventure', a spark of pure vitality. Interestingly enough, Masterman, too, predicting the future potential of the lower-middle class and the poor, comments that 'they are not afraid of life. They keep something of the adventure which takes all risks: the resolute action which cannot even see the risks it is taking'. (*COE*.118) In the novel, Leonard's 'resolute action' is his night walk: 'Leonard had reached the destination. He had visited the county of Surrey when darkness covered its amenities, and its cosy villas had re-entered ancient night. Every twelve hours this miracle happens, but he had troubled to go and see for himself.' (114) For once, Bast gets beyond books to the real thing, to 'England', and to the spirit which leads writers to write them. It is a moment of true 'culture'. The Schlegel sisters are both intensely aware of his potential, as Margaret's explanation to Henry Wilcox makes clear:

'Firstly, because he cares for physical adventure, ... Secondly, he cares for something special *in* adventure. It is quickest to call that special something poetry -'

'Oh, he's one of that writer sort.'

'No - oh no! I mean he may be, but it would be loathsome stuff. His brain is filled with the husks of books, culture - horrible; we want him to wash out his brain and go to the real thing.' (137)

Later in the same conversation, she adds; ' "He cares about adventures rightly. He's certain that our smug existence isn't all. . . . There's manhood in him as well. Yes, that's what I'm trying to say. He's a real man.' (138-9) Bast, indeed, has qualities that the liberal intellectuals with their 'feminine' values lack; they have 'culture', but they have not necessarily the vitality to 'see for themselves'. For Helen especially, later in the novel, Leonard represents a type of the true 'individual', one of 'the sort that say "I" '. (218-9) But Helen tends to idealise him, to turn him into 'a cause', while Bast, with his feet more firmly on the ground, emphasises the fundamental reality of survival: 'Death, Life and Materialism were fine words, but would Mr. Wilcox take him on as a clerk?' (223) Forster, then, sustains his realistic sense of the crucial problem of 'culture': Bast's spark of life is ineffectual because of his depressed material conditions. Nevertheless, as we shall see later on, Forster himself requires Bast's truly 'masculine' *spirit* to complete his vision of 'Liberal England' triumphant - although his seedy body he can dispense with.

The Schlegel family, especially Margaret and Helen, are the major focus of the novel. Tibby, we can define fairly easily as the effete tendency of high civilization, unwilling to work and to understand on what his cultured leisure rests; unable to relate to other people with affection; snobbish, withdrawn, supercilious, lifeless. He does not pose, and he is honest, but he is sterile:

His was the Leisure without sympathy - an attitude as fatal as the strenuous: a little cold culture may be raised on it, but no art. His sisters had seen the family danger, and had never forgotten to discount the gold islets that raised them from the sea. Tibby gave all the praise to himself, and so despised the struggling and the submerged. (289)

Tibby is an admonitory finger pointing to one of the extremes that Schlegel 'culture' can wrongly become. But it is in the sisters that much of the novel's significance resides, and they are by no means simple figures. Forster defines their background carefully: they are cosmopolitan, rather than 'English to the backbone' and provincial. Their father was a German and, considering when the novel was written, of a highly significant type:

> It was his hope that the clouds of materialism obscuring the Fatherland would part in time, and the mild intellectual light re-emerge. 'Do you imply that we Germans are stupid, Uncle Ernst?' exclaimed a haughty and magnificent nephew. Uncle Ernst replied, 'To my mind. You see the intellect, but you no longer care about it. That I call stupidity.' As the haughty nephew did not follow, he continued, 'You only care about the things that you can use, and therefore arrange them in the following order: money, supremely useful; intellect, rather useful; imagination, of no use at all. No' - for the other had protested - 'your Pan-Germanism is no more imaginative than is our Imperialism over here. It is the vice of a vulgar mind to be thrilled by bigness, to think that a thousand square miles are a thousand times more wonderful than one square mile, and that a million square miles are almost the same as heaven. That is not imagination. No, it kills it. When their poets over here try to celebrate bigness they are dead at once, and naturally. Your poets too are dying, your philosophers, your musicians to whom Europe has listened for two hundred years. Gone. Gone with the little courts that nurtured them - gone with Esterhaz and Weimar. What? What's that? Your Universities? Oh yes, you have learned men, who collect more facts than do the learned men of England. They collect facts, and facts, and empires of facts. But which of them will rekindle the light within?' (29)

The writing of *Howards End* coincides with the 'Dreadnought Crisis' and an atmosphere of international tension in which Germany was fast becoming England's bogeyman and in which, as Forster comments elsewhere in the novel, 'the remark, "England and Germany are bound to fight", renders war a little more likely each time that it is made, and is therefore made the more readily by the gutter press of either nation'. (60) Forster's choice of a cultured, liberal-humanist German background suggests, in such an atmosphere, that the *real* war, all over Europe at least, is between materialism and culture. The novel may be about 'England' and who will inherit her, but the true values are international, well beyond the chauvinistic posturings of the Wilcoxes and the Mrs. Munts and their German counterparts. And in any case, Forster's 'England' is really a beleaguered bastion of liberal-humanist civilization as a whole. Nationalistic war may come but if it does, it will be because the other conflict has already been won by the forces of materialism and barbarism. Forster recognises this quite clearly in 1908-10, and it is very much a part of the historical context which the novel contains and exists within. Such a perception is of course related to his hostility towards 'London', 'bigness', change, and the whole destructive tendency of modern life; they all threaten 'the imagination', 'the intellect' and 'the light within'. Passages like this, where the novel's theme of the conflict and reconciliation of 'materialism' and 'culture' coincides directly with its 'external' context, help to define the concept of 'history from within'. The life of the Schlegels, the Wilcoxes and so on, contains and enacts in individual terms, the vaster pressures of Forster's time - at least as he saw them.

Both daughters have inherited their father's basic values, and they are both 'advanced' young women in the context of their time. They believe in 'people', 'friends', 'personal relations'; they go to debating societies, and espouse certain causes: 'Temperance, tolerance, and sexual equality were intelligible cries to them'; and they are 'political' in the sense that 'they desired that public life should mirror whatever is good in the life within'. (27-8) On central issues they agree with each other, and are clearly complementary; but Forster draws them very differently. Helen is more of the idealist than Margaret, more passionate and impetuous. It is she who falls instantly in love with Paul Wilcox, and even more violently out again; it is she who then abhors the Wilcoxes and refuses to 'connect' with them; it is she who has a momentary affair with Leonard Bast, and has his child. Helen, like Tibby in the opposite direction, is another extreme of the Schlegel position. In some respects she is purer than Margaret: she is less dangerously tempted by the 'virtues' of Wilcoxism and by the attractions of compromise, and she has a clear and consistent vision of her principles. But she *is* idealistic, theoretic and abstract. From the beginning, Forster clearly distinguishes her in this from Margaret and while he admires her integrity, he is worried by her predilection for the abstract and theoretic. She is described as following along the lines of her sister but with 'a more irresponsible tread' (30); Margaret, later, feels 'that there [is]

74

something a little unbalanced in the mind that so readily shreds the visible', 'all vistas close in the unseen - no one doubts it - but Helen closed them rather too quickly for her taste. At every turn of speech one was confronted with reality and the absolute'. (182) The principal instance of this tendency in action, is her intense but brief relationship with Leonard Bast; it is described by Forster in significant terms: 'Helen loved the absolute. Leonard had been ruined absolutely, and had appeared to her as a man apart, isolated from the world. . . . She and the victim seemed alone in a world of unreality, and she loved him absolutely, perhaps for half an hour'. (295) It is this abstraction which worries Margaret: 'Leonard seemed not a man, but a cause. Perhaps it was Helen's way of falling in love - a curious way to Margaret . . . Helen forgot people. They were husks that had enclosed her emotion. She could pity, or sacrifice herself, or have instincts, but had she ever loved in the noblest way . . . ?' (290) When Helen brings the Basts to Evie's wedding, she does so from abstract ideas of 'justice' and 'duty', and Margaret is angry because they are remote from the actualities of the problem in hand, and cause suffering. Later, as we have noticed, Helen talks to Leonard about 'Life, Death and Materialism', while he insists that the realities are money and survival. Helen, the idealist, fails to see that to speak of the one requires the certainty of the others: ' "so never give in", continued the girl, and restated again and again the vague yet convincing plan that the Invisible lodges against the Visible. Her excitement grew as she tried to cut the rope that fastened Leonard to the earth. Woven of bitter experience it resisted her.' (222-3) Helen's principles are pure and fine in theory (and, as we shall see, Forster 'borrows' some of Helen's perceptions, and uses them as general truths in the novel,) but they represent an extreme position and their relation to the actual world is problematic. Margaret's words may finally sum up the paradox of Helen's position:

'Helen daren't slang the rich, being rich herself, but she would like to. There's an odd notion, that I haven't yet got hold of, running about at the back of her brain, that poverty is somehow 'real'. She dislikes all organization, and probably confuses wealth with the technique of wealth. Sovereigns in a stocking wouldn't bother her; cheques do. Helen is too relentless. One can't deal in her high-handed manner with the world.' (169)

Ironically, when Helen fails to give her five thousand pounds to the Basts, it is reinvested and makes her richer than she was before. (239)

It is Margaret, making 'continuous excursions' into the realms of the Visible and the Invisible, and attempting to connect them in 'proportion' (182), who is Forster's heroine. It is she who perceives the rare quality of Mrs. Wilcox, she who inherits Howards End. But she is just as much the heroine because she combines idealism with 'realism', and because she understands the importance of the Wilcoxes:

> 'If Wilcoxes hadn't worked and died in England for thousands of years, you and I couldn't sit here without having our throats cut. There would be no trains, no ships to carry us literary people about in, no fields even. Just savagery. No - perhaps not even that. Without their spirit life might never have moved out of protoplasm. More and more do I refuse to draw my income and sneer at those who guarantee it. (164)

Most importantly it is she who, within the novel, registers the liberal dilemma and so can defend the position better. After the first meeting with Leonard Bast, Margaret delivers the following speech:

> 'You and I and the Wilcoxes stand upon money as upon islands. It is so firm beneath our feet that we forget its very existence....
>
> We ought to remember, when we are tempted to criticize others, that we are standing on these islands, and that most of the others are down below the surface of the sea.... I'm tired of these rich people who pretend to be poor, and think it shows a nice mind to ignore the piles of money that keep their feet above the waves. I stand each year upon six hundred pounds, and Helen upon the same, and Tibby will stand upon eight, and as fast as our pounds crumble away into the sea they are renewed - from the sea, yes, from the sea. And all our thoughts are the thoughts of six-hundred pounders, and all our speeches; and because we don't want to steal umbrellas ourselves, we forget that below the sea people do want to steal them, and do steal them sometimes, and that what's a joke up here is down there reality -' (58-9)

Furthermore, in addition to her understanding of the relationship

76

between culture and money, Margaret is given important prophetic remarks about the liberal's diffidence and inability to decide and act - the result of his contorted consciousness of the 'muddle' of things. When the Schlegels' house is to be pulled down and they are searching for another (a 'home' for their cultural values), Margaret significantly comments: ' "We don't know what we *want*, that's the mischief with us" ' (148); and immediately afterwards: ' "I think that our race is degenerating. We cannot settle even this little thing; what will it be like when we have to settle a big one?" ' (149) In these remarks lies much of the liberal crisis. The failure to control life and mould it to one's principles - usually because the process involved seems to contradict precisely those principles - followed later by abhorrence at what *has* developed because of that failure: these are the essential characteristics of liberal impotence. It is this sort of perception on Margaret's part that leads her to acknowledge the Wilcox values. Forster makes her represent the ambivalent nature of 20th century liberal-humanism. She is aware of the central contradiction, but her sound sense of values is firmly established: 'Her conclusion was, that any human being lies nearer to the unseen than any organisation, and from this she never varied.' (30) And in 1910, if the values are inherently worthwhile, then they must - and indeed *will* - be victorious. It is Margaret who voices the optimistic note in the famous last chapter of the novel:

'Because a thing is going strong now, it need not go strong for ever,' she said. 'This craze for motion has only set in during the last hundred years. It may be followed by a civilization that won't be a movement, because it will rest on the earth. All the signs are against it now, but I can't help hoping, and very early in the morning in the garden I feel that our house is the future as well as the past.' (316)

Forster's sense of imminent change is insistent but in 1910 Margaret's vision could still be allowed to triumph. And it does: she inherits Howards End. 'The Earth' is to have one last throw.

Mrs. Wilcox, the remaining major figure in the novel, is scarcely a 'character' at all. She cannot be discussed apart from her house and what it stands for, as her first introduction suggests: 'She seemed to belong not to the young people and their motor, but to the house, and to the tree that overshadowed it. One knew that

77

she worshipped the past, and that the instinctive wisdom the past can alone bestow had descended upon her. . . .' (22) As regards 'personality' in the conventional sense, Mrs. Wilcox has little, and of vitality she has even less - especially when she is away from Howards End in London, which is where we generally see her. She only speaks passionately once, and that, significantly, is when Margaret tells her that their house is to be pulled down:

> Then she said vehemently: 'It is monstrous, Miss Schlegel; it isn't right. I had no idea that this was hanging over you. I do pity you from the bottom of my heart. To be parted from your house, your father's house - it oughtn't to be allowed. It is worse than dying. I would rather die than - Oh, poor girls! Can what they call civilization be right, if people mayn't die in the room where they were born? My dear, I am so sorry -' (79)

At Margaret's luncheon-party for 'the few delightful people' (Chapter IX), Mrs. Wilcox is a hopeless wet blanket, and it is clear that two alien ways of life are being juxtaposed. But Forster reveals in the same scene, the terms in which Mrs. Wilcox is to be regarded: 'Yet she and daily life were out of focus: one or the other must show blurred. And at lunch she seemed more out of focus than usual, and nearer the line that divides daily life from a life that may be of greater importance.' (73) Mrs. Wilcox is not really of this world; she belongs to 'the unseen'. She drifts through the book - even after her death - as the spirit of the past and of the 'culture' of Howards End. She is, we learn, of pure, traditional, English yeoman stock, intimately connected with 'the land' and her house is clearly the repository of all that is best in that tradition. But it is significantly named. Mrs. Wilcox is the very last of the Howards; her soldier brother Tom, who might have married Miss Avery, is dead, presumably killed in a colonial ('Wilcox') war. Mrs. Wilcox exists in the novel very much at the symbolic level.

Mrs. Wilcox, and what she represents, are threatened - threatened by so many of the 'modern' forces that the novel hints at: 'London', motor cars, change, movement, Wilcoxism (they have taken the paddock to build a garage), even the cultivated modernity of the Schlegel sisters. She is one of what Masterman, interestingly, also sees as 'a doomed and passing race' (*COE*.201): 'behind the appearance of a feverish prosperity and adventure - motors along all the main roads, golf-courses, gamekeepers, gardeners, armies of industrious servants, excursionists, hospitable entertainment of country house-parties - we can discern the passing of a race of men.' (*COE*.191) And Forster has an identical 'discernment'; as Mrs. Wilcox enters the modern block of flats where the Wilcoxes live in London, Margaret sees her in the following way:

> As the glass doors closed on ['the tall, lonely figure'] she had the sense of an imprisonment. The beautiful head disappeared first, still buried in the muff; the long trailing skirt followed. A woman of undefinable rarity was going up heavenward, like a specimen in a bottle. And into what a heaven - a vault as of hell, sooty black, from which soots descended! (81)

The country people at her funeral, who believe that 'London had done the mischief', declare: 'Ah, the old sort was dying out!' (84) And indeed, Mrs. Wilcox does die early in the book. Her type is clearly doomed but *the house* is not moribund. Miss Avery, the unregenerate country-woman, is alive and active ('the heart of the house [was] beating' (188)); all that is required is a suitable owner. During the Wilcox council over Mrs. Wilcox's strange 'will', Forster comments: 'To them Howards End was a house: they could not know that to her it had been a spirit, for which she sought a spiritual heir.' (94) Mrs. Wilcox, like Margaret later, had realized the economic necessity of the Wilcoxes, and had married Henry many years earlier. Margaret, in imaginative reconstruction, 'saw two women . . . one old, the other young, watching their inheritance melt away. She saw them greet him as a deliverer. "Mismanagement did it . . .". But Henry saved it; without fine feelings or deep insight, but he had saved it, and she loved him for the deed.' (192) Nevertheless, the Wilcoxes alone are not good enough. It is Margaret with her cultural values, her 'realism' and her ability to understand the modern world (Mrs. Wilcox keeps admiring this), who is to be the 'spiritual heir' and a second 'Mrs. Wilcox'. First of all, however, she needs a thorough process of preparation.

Margaret's *rites du passage* are an important feature of the novel, but they also offer an opportunity for observing the complexity of the novel's texture. *Howards End*, despite its heavily patterned and symbolic dance of 'representative' characters, is not a *simple* fable because Forster's vision is not simple. Complexity and ambivalence are, after all, part of his liberal relativism, his sense of 'muddle', of 'good-and-evil' rather than Good and Evil, (the 'Primal Curse' that Rickie suffers from in *The Longest Journey*.) Margaret, as Forster points out, makes 'innumerable false starts' (195); and she is by no means a simple, infallible vessel of the liberal-humanist ideal. She blunders almost immediately in her relationship with Mrs. Wilcox by writing her a priggish letter, and she finds her difficult to communicate with throughout their brief friendship. This is because Margaret does not yet understand what Mrs. Wilcox represents. It is significantly expressed:

> 'I thought of you as one of the early risers.'
> 'At Howards End - yes; there is nothing to get up for in London.'
> 'Nothing to get up for?' cried the scandalized Margaret. 'When there are all the autumn exhibitions, and Ysaye playing in the afternoon! Not to mention people.' (66)

Margaret's 'modernity', her love of people and her ability to survive in London, are all qualities which will be valuable to her and her inheritance, but they blunt her sensitivity to the fundamental 'value' - a love of 'the land'. Margaret achieves this much later in the book - significantly during her first visit to Howards End - and it is described in a strikingly revealing passage:

> The sense of flux which had haunted her all the year disappeared for a time. She forgot the luggage and the motor-cars, and the hurrying men who know so much and connect so little. She recaptured the sense of space, which is the basis of all earthly beauty, and, starting from Howards End, she attempted to realize England. She failed - visions do not come when we try, though they may come through trying. But an unexpected love of the island awoke in her, connecting on this side with the joys of the flesh, on that with the inconceivable. Helen and her father had known this love, poor Leonard Bast was groping after it, but it had been hidden from Margaret till this afternoon. It had certainly come through the house and old Miss Avery. Through them: the notion of 'through' persisted; her mind trembled towards a conclusion which only the unwise have put into words. Then, veering back into warmth, it dwelt on ruddy bricks, flowering plum-trees, and all the tangible joys of spring. (191)

This awareness develops in the course of the novel. At Oniton she experienced it again strongly although she was wrong to assume that this would be her 'home'. Finally, at Howards End, 'the peace of the country was entering into her'. (293) As this education proceeds, Margaret comes increasingly to resemble Mrs. Wilcox.

Another of Margaret's 'false starts' is in her relationship with Leonard Bast, (Helen is implicated in this, too). She simply does not understand him or his attitudes to life. Only gradually does she acquire a sense that poverty makes people think differently: 'Margaret really minded, for it gave her a glimpse into squalor. To trust people is a luxury in which only the wealthy can indulge; the poor cannot afford it'. (35) Rightly or wrongly, Margaret's perception has changed. Nevertheless, she still fails to understand that, for Bast, she and Helen represent 'Romance', a sacred retreat from the squalor of his everyday life, and that by attempting to break out of the former into the latter she is blundering badly. (See pp. 115-6 and Chapter XVI). Indeed her interference over the matter of his job has serious *actual* repercussions, in that Bast's already uncertain material position is totally demolished. As the book progresses, Margaret's understanding of the realities of the Bast world increases, especially after the events at Evie's wedding. But she still fails, finally, to come to terms with what it represents, and is only able to comprehend Leonard as 'the spirit of adventure'. That, however, is Forster's problem too, and I will return to it.

The most complex aspect of Margaret's 'preparation' lies in her relationship to the Wilcoxes. Despite her recognition of the 'necessity' of the Wilcox values if her own are to survive and flourish, Margaret's are established as the fundamentally important ones. This is made quite clear early in the novel:

'The truth is that there is a great outer life that you and I have never touched - a life in which telegrams and anger count. Personal relations, that we think supreme, are not supreme there. . . . But here's my difficulty. This outer life, though obviously horrid, often seems the real one - there's grit in it. It does breed character. Do personal relations lead to sloppiness in the end?'

'Oh, Meg, that's what I felt, only not so clearly, when the Wilcoxes were so competent, and seemed to have their hands on all the ropes.'

'Don't you feel it now?'

'I remember Paul at breakfast,' said Helen quietly. 'I shall never forget him. He had nothing to fall back upon. I know that

personal relations are the real life, for ever and ever.'
  'Amen!' (27)

But Forster does not leave it that simple. There is a fatal attractive-
ness about the Wilcoxes, their manners and attitudes, which both
sisters respond to. They both, at times, enjoy being told that their
'advanced' opinions are 'nonsense' or idealistic or 'typically
female', and they have a certain respect for Wilcox efficiency.
Helen gets over hers with the end of the Paul affair; Margaret, however, with her pragmatic evaluation of the Wilcoxes' place in the
order of things, can envisage a less passionate but mutually satis-
fying relationship with Henry. Much of the novel's subtlety and
maturity of perception resides in the complexity of the Margaret/
Henry relationship. Most importantly, perhaps, Forster uses it to
reveal the dangers of her pragmatism. In her willingness to coun-
tenance 'Wilcoxism', Margaret is tainted; she is not, in fact, presented as a pure vessel of the liberal-humanist ideal, but comes close
to betraying her own values. This, and hence her open-eyed acceptance of Henry, are integral parts of her character. Her danger is
apparent, first of all, in the scene, shortly after her engagement to
Henry, when Helen argues passionately about their 'responsibility'
for Bast's leaving the Porphyrion Insurance Company on Henry's
'careless' advice. Margaret, torn between fiancé and sister, eases
the explosive situation by removing Henry. She fails to face the
issues. This is emphasised by her behaviour when Helen brings the
Basts to the wedding at Oniton:

> She was ashamed of her own diplomacy. In dealing with a Wil-
> cox, how tempting it was to lapse from comradeship, and to
> give him the kind of woman he desired! . . . Now she understood
> why some women prefer influence to rights. Mrs. Plynlimmon,
> when condemning suffragettes, had said: 'The woman who
> can't influence her husband to vote the way she wants ought to
> be ashamed of herself.' Margaret had winced, but she was in-
> fluencing Henry now, and though pleased at her little victory,
> she knew that she had won it by the methods of the harem. (214)

Her whole tendency is to 'silence' the affair. In her love for Henry,
and equally in her love for Oniton which she, *wrongly*, believes is
to be her future home, she is 'practical', she covers up, is rather
careless of the Basts, and dismissive of Henry's irresponsibility:

'it was not her tragedy: it was Mrs. Wilcox's'. (218) But she too, soon, is to be 'Mrs. Wilcox'. Margaret is close, at this point, to blinding herself in one eye, to seeing 'steadily', rather than 'whole'. Not surprisingly, we learn later, Helen thought that the notes Margaret wrote to Leonard and herself at 'the George' in Oniton, were dictated by Henry Wilcox. (291)

Margaret's danger from compromising her own values reaches its crisis towards the end of the book, with Helen's 'visit' to Howards End, her pregnancy and her wish to stay in the house overnight. Margaret connives at Henry Wilcox's plan to trap Helen, discover her 'secret', and carry her off to 'a specialist'. Forster describes it as their 'hunting expedition to Howards End' (298), which 'drew its ethics from the wolf-pack'. (265) Margaret is clearly implicated: 'Sick at heart, Margaret joined in the chase. She wrote her sister a lying letter, *at her husband's dictation*. (265. My italics.) She is herself aware of the infection; when Henry tries to leave her behind, 'she said not a single word: he was only treating her as she had treated Helen, and her rage at his dishonesty only helped to indicate what Helen would feel against them. She thought, "I deserve it: I am punished for lowering my colours." ' (267-8) For a moment the delicate relationship with her sister is jeopardised. Helen says, when they finally meet: ' "one loses faith in everything after this" ' (272); and Margaret asks forgiveness: 'she had to purge a greater crime than any that Helen could have committed - that want of confidence that is the work of the devil'. (273) 'Panic and emptiness' were imminent but Margaret has, of course, saved herself by deserting the pack and rejoining her sister; the life of values is reaffirmed. Much earlier, Forster had written: 'There are moments when the inner life actually "pays", when years of self-scrutiny, conducted for no ulterior motive, are suddenly of practical use'. (182) This, for the sisters, surrounded by their possessions and at Howards End, is such a moment: 'And all the time their salvation was lying round them - the past sanctifying the present; the present, with wild heart-throb, declaring that there would after all be a future, with laughter and the voices of children. . . . The inner life had paid.' (278) It is significant that out of this recrudescence of integrity should spring Margaret's reference to Mrs. Bast in Henry's presence, and her attempt to make him 'see' the connection between his own past behaviour and Helen's. No longer does she protect him and so betray her own values by accepting those of the Wilcoxes.

Margaret's relationship with Henry, finally, is itself an example of Forster's sensitive apprehension of the complexity of the 'connections' he is concerned to make. Not only does Henry affect *her*, as we have seen above, ('he did alter her character - a little. There was . . . a social pressure that would have her think conjugally,' (164)) but even her effect on him is less than simple and successful. For much of their relationship, Margaret believes that she will be able to change him, to develop his 'undeveloped heart', remake his 'inner life', make him 'connect': 'she connected . . . and she hoped some day Henry would do the same' (194); 'she had abandoned any plan of action. Love is the best, and the more she let herself love him, the more chance was there that he would set his soul in order. . . . Disappointed a hundred times, she still hoped' (205); and later, in her moral confusion and 'silence' over the Jacky Bast affair, she reflects: 'Henry must have it as he liked, for she loved him, and some day she would use her love to make him a better man'. (227) But Forster, with much greater 'realism', has warned us earlier that Margaret's hopes are doomed to failure:

> Mature as he was, she might yet be able to help him to the building of the rainbow bridge that should connect the prose in us with the passion. Without it we are meaningless fragments, half monks, half beasts, unconnected arches that have never joined into a man. . . . She would only point out the salvation that was latent in his own soul, and in the soul of every man. Only connect! That was the whole of her sermon. Only connect the prose and the passion, and both will be exalted, and human love will be seen at its height. Live in fragments no longer. Only connect, and the beast and the monk, robbed of the isolation that is life to either, will die. . . . By quiet indications the bridge would be built and span their lives with beauty.
>
> But she failed. For there was one quality in Henry for which she was never prepared, however much she reminded herself of it: his obtuseness. He simply did not notice things, and there was no more to be said. (174-5)

After the failure of her passionate attempt to make him 'see' the connection between his 'affair' and Helen's (287), Margaret too despairs of helping him: 'Though he would build up his life without hers, she could not apologise. He had refused to connect, on the clearest issue that can be laid before a man, and their love must take the consequences.' (309) Forster, and now Margaret, have realised the recalcitrance of the Wilcoxes, and the weakness of 'Love'. It is a courageous and significant perception of the liberal-humanist's position, and the subtlety and ambivalence of Margaret's relationship with Henry contributes, with her other 'false starts', to the solidity of the book's realisation of its world-view. The fact that Forster himself 'borrows' Margaret's 'sermon' - 'Only connect . . .' - as the epigraph for the whole novel and successfully forges the 'connections' at the end *despite the failure of Love* reveals a deeper ambivalence which the novel contains.

What, then, is Forster making *Howards End* say? The novel proposes that the traditional owners of England are being dis-possessed, and that the new heirs should be furnished with the best possible values and advantages for assuring the survival and vitality of the traditional culture. But Forster recognises both that there are powerful forces inimical to it, and that the new 'heirs' will be modern, that they will not necessarily be 'English to the backbone', nor will they be the product of one social group. The necessary 'connections' have to be established between certain diverse, but indispensable, factors. At the abstract level, these are defined as 'the passion' and 'the prose', the 'inner' and the 'outer' lives, the ability to see life 'steadily' and the ability to see it 'whole', (where Henry wishes to 'Concentrate', Margaret wishes to 'Con-nect'). To put it another way, which Forster himself almost makes explicit, there is to be a connection between the 'male' and 'female' virtues. Margaret, early on, senses that their house is 'irrevocably feminine, even in father's time', and that the Wilcoxes' is 'irrevoc-ably masculine'. Both have weaknesses which their owners must struggle against: the former against 'effeminacy', the latter against 'brutality'. (43) The dissociation of the 'virtues' is clearly un-natural, and it is equally clear that they would be mutually forti-fying in association. These abstractions, however, have, within the novel, individual and social definition. Let us consider again the various strands: Mrs. Wilcox, the spirit of 'Liberal England' and of 'the Past', inhabits Howards End/England, but is about to leave it. That is the basic situation. But who is it to be left to? The most suitable heirs are the Schlegel sisters, of part-German origin but possessing the right values - idealism, a belief in 'personal relations', passion, culture, and so on. Of the two, Margaret is the more down to earth, and she is the true *'spiritual* heir'. But she recognises the need for a solid material base - 'the great outer life of telegrams and anger' (27) - on which to establish and propagate their values. This the Wilcoxes supply but they lack any sort of inner life, they are all 'prose' and no 'poetry', public people whose innermost reality is 'panic and emptiness'. Howards End/England cannot be left to them, but equally Margaret cannot inherit it alone, because she cannot survive without material and physical support. As part of Margaret's preparation for inheritance, therefore, she has to marry Henry Wilcox and become a new 'Mrs. Wilcox', so inheriting 'the house' on the basis of a connection between money and culture. Thus a base is secured. But who is the *actual* heir? Margaret does 'not love children. . . . I can play with their beauty and charm, but that is all - nothing real, not one scrap of what there ought to be'. (314) And Henry is too old and broken. Obviously Money and Culture are not enough; they leave too much out, and in particular the vital spark of life itself. The real heir, protected by the values already defined, is the child of Helen and Leonard Bast's union - a union, it is worth noticing, between two complementary representatives of the *middle classes* alone. Helen's passion and idealism 'connect' with the spirit of 'adventure' and of unquenchable individual life in Leonard - that potential for true 'wholeness' of culture hinted at, but unborn, in him and the huge class he represents. Unable to break out of the imprisoning poverty of his own life, Bast cannot achieve full being, but his son and Helen's - given money and the 'life of values' - will be able to achieve this. The new heir of Howards End/England, then, is an amalgam of all the essential forces, with Margaret and her liberal-humanist culture as a sort of Regent. Hence Forster's imperative: 'Only connect . . .'.

All this, then, may be taken as the novel's 'historical' significance at the 'conscious' or 'authorial' level: the way in which through character, plot, action, pattern and so forth an historical situation is expressed. It is not, of course, a history of events or 'great men', but an attempt to recreate what Raymond Williams calls 'a structure of feeling' as it is revealed by ordinary people acting out the ordinary business of their lives. What *is* enacted is Forster's vision, in 1910, of traditional Liberal England, beset by dangerous, destructive forces, finally prevailing through a realistic, 'modern' liberal-humanism, which makes 'connections' with other powerful, supportive forces, and leavens them with its values.

But it is precisely on the point of the victorious 'vision' that another type of analysis is required which may reveal the second, 'unconscious', significance of the book, and another type of understanding. There are certain questions posed by the curiously ambivalent effect of *Howards End,* which require consideration and answer: How is the 'vision' victorious? How are the 'connections' achieved? Is the movement of the book 'convincing'? Is the 'realism' sustained? The answers to these questions lie in the analysis of ostensibly 'literary' matters, the novel's rhetoric both linguistic and structural. We shall find, in fact, that the least accessible 'historical' level of the book's total 'statement' is contained in precisely these formal dimensions.

Let us begin with the base of the vision itself: 'Liberal England'. The England which Forster cherishes is actually that which I have suggested the Georgian poets described and eulogised: 'pastoral' England, an idealised and largely literary myth. (Forster himself, much later in his life, admitted that he carried 'a ruck-sack of traditional nature emotions' (*TC*.361); and the opening paragraphs of his essay on the rural poet William Barnes (*TC*.208), suggest his 'Georgian' proclivities.) This is not to deny that the English countryside can be idyllic, merely to suggest that the idyll is partial and exclusive because it ignores other aspects of rural life, let alone anything else. Forster's ideal England is itself something of a 'poetical reality', and is not unlike that which Brooke was evoking in 'Grantchester'. One can refer to the famous opening paragraph of Chapter XIX, with its undisguised rhetoric:

If one wanted to show a foreigner England, perhaps the wisest course would be to take him to the final section of the Purbeck Hills, and stand him on their summit, a few miles to the east of Corfe. Then system after system of our island would roll together under his feet. Beneath him is the valley of the Frome, and all the wild lands that come tossing down from Dorchester, black and gold, to mirror their gorse in the expanses of Poole. The valley of the Stour is beyond, unaccountable stream, dirty at Blandford, pure at Wimborne - the Stour, sliding out of fat fields, to marry the Avon beneath the tower of Christchurch. The valley of the Avon - invisible, but far to the north the trained eye may see Clearbury Ring that guards it, and the imagination may leap beyond that on to Salisbury Plain itself, and beyond the Plain to all the glorious downs of Central England. Nor is Suburbia absent. Bournemouth's ignoble coast cowers to the right, heralding the pine-trees that mean, for all their beauty, red houses, and the Stock Exchange, and extend to the gates of London itself. So tremendous is the City's trail! But the cliffs of Freshwater it shall never touch, and the island will guard the Island's purity till the end of time. Seen from the west, the Wight is beautiful beyond all laws of beauty. It is as if a fragment of England floated forward to greet the foreigner - chalk of our chalk, turf of our turf, epitome of what will follow. (156-7)

What is interesting here, apart from the poetic language, is the recognition of 'Suburbia' and 'the City's trail', followed by the significant shift into the future imperative tense - 'the cliffs of Freshwater it *shall* never touch'. This is simply a rhetorical flourish, without a rational base, and it might well be described as shouting to keep one's courage up. The novel is studded with passages of a similar nature in which the most noteworthy features are the caressing tone and the general imprecision of the language:

In these English farms, if anywhere, one might see life steadily and see it whole, group in one vision its transitoriness and its eternal youth, connect - connect without bitterness until all men are brothers. (250)

Here men had been up since dawn. Their hours were ruled, not by a London office, but by the movements of the crops and the sun. That they were men of the finest type only the sentimentalist can declare. But they kept to the life of daylight. They are England's hope. Clumsily they carry forward the torch of the sun, until such time as the nation sees fit to take it up. Half-clodhopper, half board-school prig, they can still throw back to a nobler stock, and breed yeomen. (301)

Hertfordshire is England at its quietest, with little emphasis of river and hill; it is England meditative. If Drayton were with us again to write a new edition of his incomparable poem, he would sing the nymphs of Hertfordshire as indeterminate of feature, with hair obfuscated by the London smoke. Their eyes would be sad, and averted from their fate towards the Northern flats, their leader not Isis or Sabrina, but the slowly flowing Lea. No glory of raiment would be theirs, no urgency of dance; but they would be real nymphs. (185)

The problem with this pleasant image is that it is an idealisation, and Forster's reliance on smooth cadences and vague rhetoric to bolster it, reveals how insubstantial the vision is. In the second passage above, he attempts to pre-empt the accusation of 'sentimentality' by mentioning it himself, but the imprecision and indulgent tone of phrases like 'they kept to the life of daylight', 'a nobler stock', 'England's hope', 'the torch of the sun', idealise and blur the subject. But a vision such as this is necessarily vague and imprecise, because its *ability* to idealise relies, simply, on the exclusion of all those aspects of England which it cannot assimilate. The Georgian poets were past-masters at this, and Forster is guilty of it too. There is a tell-tale sign in the last passage quoted above: 'Their eyes would be sad, and averted from their fate . . .'. An 'averting of the eyes' is one way of describing the Georgian view of England and for Forster, too, 'these English farms' are more essentially 'England' than are London and the great towns - even in 1910. Masterman, despite his own love of 'the earth', is very much more realistic than Forster:

> But no one to-day would seek in the ruined villages and dwindling population of the countryside the spirit of an 'England' four-fifths of whose people have now crowded into the cities. The little red-roofed towns and hamlets, the labourer in the fields at noontide or evening, the old English service in the old English village church, now stand but as the historical survival of a once great and splendid past. Is 'England' then to be discovered in the feverish industrial energy of the manufacturing cities? In the vast welter and chaos of the capital of Empire? Amongst the new Plutocracy? The middle classes? The artisan populations? The broken poor? All contribute their quota to the stream of the national life. (*COE*.12)

The real danger of Forster's vision is that large areas of 'England's' life and culture are dismissed as in some way 'unreal'. He excludes or neutralises dynamic, even if disruptive, aspects of society in favour of 'the past'. I do not, of course, mean that Forster *should* have written about mining or public-houses or factories or football or Pasteur or Marconi or the diet of the working class; simply that there is a *dismissive* tone in his treatment of even those insistent realities that he is concerned with. London, for all its symbolic status, is dismissed as not 'England'. If we return to the long passage from the opening of Chapter XIII discussed at the beginning of this book, and look again at the second paragraph, we will see how Forster's passive despair makes the description general and reductive. The phrase 'no pulsation of humanity' in London, suggests a detachment that is really an elitist and alienated ignorance: 'as I am out of tune with this place, it cannot be good'[3]. It is symptomatic of a fundamental blind-spot in the liberal-humanist consciousness that it assumes its own values, its own form of 'civilisation', are absolute and for all time and that culture is static having achieved its apotheosis in the liberal-humanist image. Later in the novel, Margaret has an 'epiphany' of London: 'The mask fell off the city, and she saw it for what it really is - a caricature of infinity. The familiar barriers, the streets along which she moved, the houses between which she had made her little journeys for so many years, became negligible suddenly.' (261) 'For what it really *is*': had this been Margaret's reflection alone, the verb would have been 'was', not 'is'. Once again the phrase implies Forster's Olympian rejection of the alien force. 'London' does not fit into 'Liberal England', but if one has the right values it can be dismissed, is 'negligible suddenly'. Hence the rhetoric.

The same dismissive tendency is apparent in Forster's treatment of the lower classes. Unlike Masterman, who devotes two sections to the 'very poor', Forster regards them as 'unthinkable' and therefore, 'we are not concerned with the very poor'. This is not simple callousness; it is an honest admission that he knows nothing at all about them. And it is Forster's right as a novelist to delimit his objectives, to refuse to deal with them. All we may do is to note that in a novel which seems to be concerned with the condition and future of England, the poor do not appear. It could, of course, be argued that the novel is only concerned with the condition of the middle classes, and not with 'England' after all. But this would both fail to take account of much of its imagery and reference ('English farms', 'English houses', English trees', etc), and would reinforce the exclusiveness of the liberal 'future'. Even if the middle classes set their own house in order, solidly founded on the 'life of values', and establish a powerful enclave within society, they cannot be discrete; they must be related to other groups and forces. And if their values are to permeate and inform society, the means of 'transmitting' private values into public good remains to be discovered. Willy-nilly, a novel concerned with the state of the middle classes in the early years of this century, is concerned with 'England', and Forster was too perceptive an intelligence to be unaware of it. Nevertheless, he did not deal with 'the very poor'.

The case of the Basts is rather different, and Forster *is* concerned to include them, and the class they represent, in the 'new England'. But as characters, they are clearly 'created', rather than known and observed. Jacky is one of the few really wooden caricatures in all of Forster's fiction and significantly she is little more than a necessary agent in the plot and pattern of the novel. Leonard is better, but he is still not convincing. He is *described* by Forster, rather than presented dramatically and even when he is allowed to express himself, it is clearly in the terms that Forster *thought* a man like that would think:

> 'I'll tell you another thing too. I care a good deal about improving myself by means of Literature and Art, and so getting a wider outlook. For instance, when you came in I was reading Ruskin's *Stones of Venice*. I don't say this to boast, but just to show you the kind of man I am. I can tell you I enjoyed that classical concert this afternoon.' (52)

The Basts are poorly-drawn characters, which suggests again that Forster is not very familiar with the class or its life style. But what is more significant is the tone he adopts when discussing Leonard as 'representative' of his class, especially at the opening of Chapter VI:

> The boy, Leonard Bast, stood at the extreme verge of gentility. He was not in the abyss, but he could see it, and at times people whom he knew had dropped in, and counted no more. He knew that he was poor, and would admit it: he would have died sooner than confess any inferiority to the rich. This may be splendid of him. But he was inferior to most rich people, there is not the least doubt of it. He was not as courteous as the average rich man, nor as intelligent nor as healthy, nor as lovable. His mind and his body had been alike underfed,

because he was poor, and because he was modern they were always craving better food. Had he lived some centuries ago, in the brightly coloured civilizations of the past, he would have had a definite status, his rank and his income would have corresponded. But in his day the angel of Democracy had arisen, enshadowing the classes with leathern wings, and proclaiming, 'All men are equal - all men, that is to say, who possess umbrellas', and so he was obliged to assert gentility, lest he slipped into the abyss where nothing counts, and the statements of Democracy are inaudible. (44)

It is again the detachment, and the condescension, which constitute the dismissal: the lack of understanding implies the absence of anything worthwhile to understand. If Leonard could stop being 'poor', he would be 'lovable'; as it is, his class's 'culture' can be understood but not appreciated. And 'Democracy', a liberal article of faith surely, is, *in practice,* guilty of engendering this 'inferior' culture. The unconscious *elitism* of the Liberal position could not be better expressed than in the distaste this passage reveals for *the actual* results of its abstract principles. Forster's attitude to Bast, as the story develops, would seem to be that if his miserable being can be disregarded or eradicated, then his 'spirit' will be invaluable. As for Helen, Bast is more a 'cause' than a man and Forster has to kill him off to make his presence in 'Liberal England' possible.

My general point, however, is that any vision of 'England' in the early 20th century which cannot or will not contain such realities as London or the huge battalions of the system's 'prisoners', is partial to the point of being invalid. Indeed, the most revealing omission in *Howards End* is a detailed and extensive portrayal of the forces opposed to the realisation of the vision. To be just to Forster, he constantly hints at the vulnerability of the vision: 'London was but a foretaste of this nomadic civilization which is altering human nature so profoundly' (243); ' "And London is only part of something else, I'm afraid. Life's going to be melted down, all over the world." Margaret knew that her sister spoke truly.' (316) Nevertheless, the overall movement and texture of the novel do not embody this. It is withheld by the 'positive' vision. For realities as potent as the forces of destructive change are suggested to be, they are scarcely realised in the world the novel defines. Sometimes they are the vague fears of the narrative voice or its representatives; sometimes they are the passing utterances of characters in conversation; at other times, they are presented symbolically: 'London', or the motor-cars that cover things with dust and kill cats. Many of the insistent realities of Edwardian life - suburban spread, Socialism, female suffrage, Anglo-German hostility, urban living, speed, change - hang in the air, but they are not allowed to obtrude. This is partly, no doubt, a result of the contemporary 'Satisfaction' which we noticed earlier - the 'prophetic' tendencies of a period are always much clearer in retrospect - but it is also a result of the basic uncertainty of the vision. To allow full status to such elements would *ipso facto* destroy the myth of 'Liberal England'. They are fundamentally antithetical to it. So if the vision is to be achieved, forces hostile to it must be made to seem less formidable than they are in reality. This is not to suggest that Forster is incapable of 'realistic writing'. On the contrary, much of *Howards End* is brilliantly realistic. It is simply to suggest that by omitting to give full realisation to certain important aspects of the real world, Forster tacitly admits that his vision could not accommodate them. It represents, in fictional form, the liberal tendency to disconnect culture from society while still considering it to have a crucial social function: 'values' independent of a particular historical location.

In itself, the basis of the vision, 'Liberal England', is something of a myth. But at the same time, the whole movement of the book affirms the validity of it: Howards End survives, and is inherited by suitable heirs who have themselves managed to 'connect'. As Virginia Woolf early remarked: in Forster's work as a whole and in *Howards End* especially, 'there is a vision which he is determined that we shall see' (*CEI*.345); 'we are tapped on the shoulder. We are to notice this, to take heed of that. Margaret or Helen, we are made to understand, is not speaking simply as herself; her words have another and a larger intention. So, exerting ourselves to find out the meaning, we step from the enchanted world of imagination, where our faculties work freely, to the twilight world of theory, where only our intellect functions dutifully.' (349) In other words, this is a legislative rather than a descriptive work; it says, for instance, who the inheritors of 'England' *ought to be*, not who they *are*. *Howards End* is, in fact, a socio-moral fable although the world the novel defines *purports* to be realistic, empirically perceived, equivalent to 'the world out there'. The 'correct' resolution is known before the book begins and Forster's task is to ensure that this is actually effected. Much of the novel, therefore, is an artificial justification of the final 'vision'; every scene of domestic comedy, every conversation, every event, every word, is controlled by its demands. As Virginia Woolf again noted: 'he never loses himself or forgets himself for long in sheer delight in the beauty or the interest of things as they are.' (349) How far any novelist conveys 'things as they are' (although it is often assumed that this is what the realist can do) is a debatable point. Nevertheless, Virginia Woolf's comment points to Forster's limited interest in 'felt life' (we may recall his comments about 'the visionary writer' in his essay on Forrest Reid referred to above), and to his primary concern with putting flesh on the 'vision'. The patterned unity of his novels is controlled from without; it is the force of an *idea* which creates it. All the major novelists of the realistic tradition have, of course, revealed a view of life in their works - the ideological hand guides; how could it not? - but it is implicit in the densely-worked 'social world' of their novels. An extrinsic moral position may be *discovered* in the complex web of intensely analysed and vividly realised social relationships but it is not imposed on them so that they *must* act according to it. Perhaps the distinction is that where they reveal an idea *in* life, Forster proposes an idea *about* life. In the past, novelists had, in different ways, regarded the world as there to be understood, whereas Forster, given his time and cast of mind, had to project an image of what it ought to be.

Despite the discernment and subtlety, the irony, the anti-pompous and sceptical tentativeness of *Howards End's* style and manner, there is a resolute controlling mechanism which makes the novel 'prove' Forster's conception; the material is cut and sewn to the approved design. Paradoxically, Forster was well aware of the problems of the over-patterned novel, and although he is criticising Henry James in terms of aesthetic, rather than moral, control, his comments in *Aspects of the Novel* suggest something of his own tendency:

It is this question of the rigid pattern . . . Can it be combined with the immense richness of material which life provides? Wells and James would agree it cannot. Wells would go on to

94

say that life should be given the preference, and must not be whittled or distended for a pattern's sake. My own prejudices are with Wells. . . . That then is the disadvantage of a rigid pattern. It may externalise the atmosphere, spring naturally from the plot, but it shuts the doors on life, and leaves the novelist doing exercises, generally in the drawing room. (*AN*.164-5)

If Forster's prejudices were with Wells' ostensible openness to life, his practice was equally close to the didactic realism of Wells' fiction. But Forster might have added that pattern does not just exclude life, but can actually falsify the 'life' it is treating.

Howards End, however, is a complex work, and there remains a major complication: the novel is, of course, by no means unequivocally a 'fable' or a 'romance'. As critics from Virginia Woolf onwards have noticed,[4] the novel is a mixture. The problems develop when the expectations of a realistic novel are aroused, and in *Howards End* they certainly are. The conversational opening of the novel: 'One may as well begin with Helen's letters to her sister' (5), with the letters appended, immediately suggests a novel aiming at verisimilitude. Forster continues throughout to be specific about time and place. The references to Tariff Reform, Imperialism, female emancipation, the NEAC, Augustus John, suburban spread and so on, quite clearly establish the scene as Edwardian England between about 1908 and 1910. Equally carefully established - if sometimes not very knowledgeably - are the social matrices of the various characters: their heredity, class, attitudes, work, houses, etc. The Basts' 'background', for example, is attempted in considerable detail, and the treatment of their flat reads more like Arnold Bennett or H. G. Wells than 'romance':

The sitting-room contained, besides the arm-chair, two other chairs, a piano, a three-legged table, and a cosy corner. Of the walls, one was occupied by the window, the other by a draped mantleshelf bristling with Cupids. Opposite the window was the door and beside the door a bookcase, while over the piano there extended one of the masterpieces of Maud Goodman. (46)

Great care is taken, also, with the characterisation and the dialogue. The former is, admittedly, done largely through the narrative voice, but then this, rather than the dramatic mode, has been the norm for most of the realist tradition. It is particularly strong in the cases of the Wilcoxes and the Schlegels, and when Forster does present a dramatic 'scene', the dialogue is generally handled in a masterly way and is entirely convincing both in the comic and the serious vein. Margaret's luncheon party for Mrs. Wilcox (Chapter IX) is a good example of the former, and Henry's 'confession' to Margaret about his affair with Jacky Bast, of the latter:

'Did Helen come?' she asked.

He shook his head.

'But that won't do at all, at all! We don't want her gossiping with Mrs. Bast.'

'Good God! no!' he exclaimed, suddenly natural. Then he caught himself up. 'Let them gossip. My game's up, though I thank you for your unselfishness - little as my thanks are worth.' . . .

'It is not good,' said Henry. 'Those things leak out; you cannot stop a story once it has started. I have known cases of other men - I despised them once, I thought that *I'm* different, *I* shall never be tempted. Oh, Margaret - ' He came and sat down near by, improvising emotion. She could not bear to listen to him. 'We fellows all come to grief once in our time. Will you believe that? There are moments when the strongest man - "Let him who standeth, take heed lest he fall." That's true, isn't it? If you knew all, you would excuse me. I was far from good influences - far even from England. I was very, very lonely, and longed for a woman's voice. That's enough. I have told you too much already for you to forgive me now.' (229)

What Forster is so good at doing in scenes of this sort, is making a 'thematic' concern take on the *timbre* of an actual conversation: the revelation here, in the tones and postures of Henry's speech, of what Helen has earlier identified as the 'panic and emptiness' at the heart of 'Wilcoxism', is brilliantly achieved. But even when the characterisation is weak - as in the case of the Basts - it is rather because Forster does not *know* about them, than because he is not *trying* to make them 'convincing'. The very amount of effort he clearly puts into describing them suggests this.

Finally, one further aspect of the 'realistic' texture of large sections of *Howards End* is the wry wisdom of the authorial comment. Except in certain ways, which I will explain in a moment, this is both common to the realistic tradition and, in Lionel Trilling's apt word about Forster's wisdom, indelibly 'worldly'[5]. For example:

The two men were gradually assuming the manner of the committee-room. They were both at their best when serving on committees. They did not make the mistake of handling human affairs in the bulk, but disposed of them item by item, sharply. . . . It is the best - perhaps the only - way of dodging emotion. They were the average human article, and had they considered the note as a whole it would have driven them miserable or mad. Considered item by item, the emotional content was minimised, and all went forward smoothly. (93)

Such passages are the result of observation and reflection, the quality which makes Forster's essays so continuously stimulating. They imply the 'realism' he admires in Margaret Schlegel: 'a profound vivacity, a continual and sincere response to all that she encountered in her path through life'. (11) It is precisely this complex and ironic perception of life which opposes the more rhetorical or vision-controlled passages, so that despite their common theme, each calls into question the other's validity.

There would be little excuse in labouring what is perhaps an obvious point about Forster's realism, were it not that several aspects of the novel run counter to it and that the novel as a whole implicitly rejects it in favour of 'vision'. The 'precarious synthesis' that David Lodge mentions, of realism, romance and allegory (see above p.14), is upset by Forster's conflicting needs. On the one hand, he wishes to propagate a vision - which he partially recognises to be exclusive and insecure - and for which he needs myth, pattern, symbolism: 'contrived' or 'fabulous' modes. On the other hand, he must try and convince us of the 'reality' of the vision: one can scarcely hope to make 'England' credible if one ignores England. And for this he needs all the paraphernalia of realism, since the danger of plain fable, because of its manifest artificiality, is the option it grants the reader simply to disregard its 'moral'. But because the vision itself is partial, the realistic bolstering of it never really becomes credible; it is too closely tied to the symbolic and mythic elements and is too regulated and selective. Forster's eye is first and foremost on the 'vision', and the 'realism' exists, therefore, in terms of that. The mixed mode of *Howards End* is never quite synthesis. As Virginia Woolf remarked: 'Elaboration, skill, wisdom,

97

penetration, beauty - they are all there, but they lack fusion; they lack cohesion; the book as a whole lacks force. His gifts in their variety and number tend to trip each other up.' (*CEI*.348) Those critics who have attempted to justify Forster's 'romance' or 'visionary' apparatus, in this novel at least, as appropriate to his didactic purposes, fail to recognise that the partial realism involves not just questions about literary coherence or 'decorum', but also questions about the validity of the 'vision' itself. A vision or a fable has to be absolute, totalising and assured; tiny fragments of doubt, or chinks through which an alternative world can be perceived, are likely to smash its all-embracing completeness. It must exist totally within the artificial but absolute walls of its convention. Forster's liberal vision is, almost by its nature, tentative and uncertain; 'realism' creeps in, the certainty of the world of the fable is questioned, and the realistic elements in the novel set up a clamour for more *proof*, more application of vision to world. The walls have been breached and when such fissures appear an affirmation has to be made in symbolic or mythical terms. This uncertainty is significantly less evident in the earlier novels where the social satire is firmly contained within the terms of the moral vision - Life against non-Life. But in *Howards End*, where the vision is to comprehend a social reality - England - the strains begin to show. The correlation between liberal dilemma and fictional form is most apparent here; just as the insistent realities of the real world undermine the liberal position so that it must begin to doubt itself, so the realistic elements in the novel call in question the self-sufficiency of the fable, and thus the validity of the vision.

Were this paradox - vision juxtaposed with reality - the novel's intended subject, consciously realised and explored in the characters and the action, then the novel would be less questionable, less synthetic, less 'finished'. There would be no need for the 'positive' ending which reveals intensive structuring on behalf of the controlling idea. But the paradox is not a 'subject' *within Howards End*; the *whole novel* is constructed to confirm the uncertain absolute of the vision. From the beginning, it is geared to proving the *idea*, and prove it it does. The novel attempts, to borrow Margaret's thoughts quoted at the beginning of this chapter, to reflect 'the chaotic nature of our daily life', but it is finally bound by the 'orderly sequence' of Forster's vision and its narrative formulation. In the search for harmony, for 'connection', narrative and stylistic contrivance is used to justify them against other, more realistic, elements that the novel's world itself contains.

It is to these 'contrivances' that we must now turn. There are two features in particular I wish to consider which help to create the fictive 'completeness' of *Howards End* - the plot and the narrative voice; and a third in passing, the use of symbolism. In the first case, it is what may be called the controlled contingency of the plot which is most obviously used to make certain that the right things happen and that the vision is given substance. And it is worth bearing in mind Forster's remarks about Hardy's use of plot in this context. (See above, p.60) The main 'connection' in the plot is the Wilcox/Schlegel relationship, and this is set up perfectly convincingly: they have met abroad, and the sisters have been invited to stay at Howards End. Helen goes; Margaret is unable to, because Tibby is ill. The novel opens with this, and with the furore surrounding Helen's abortive 'love-affair' with Paul Wilcox. But the next major event is the chance encounter with Leonard Bast at the Beethoven concert, and Helen's 'theft' of his umbrella. This, too, is effectively done; it is only later, when the extraordinary web of connections it implies, emerges - especially that of Jacky Bast and Henry Wilcox - that the coincidence registers its full force. The following chapter fills in the Bast 'background'. But the next one opens: ' "Oh Margaret", cried her aunt next morning, "such a most unfortunate thing has happened." ' (54) The 'most unfortunate thing' is that the Wilcoxes have, by chance, come to live in the flats immediately opposite their house. From this develops the friendship between Margaret and Mrs. Wilcox, 'which', the next chapter begins, in characteristically Forsterian fashion, 'was to develop so quickly.' (61) They project a trip to Howards End, but just as they are boarding the train at Kings Cross, Evie and Henry - supposedly motoring in Yorkshire - appear. The fortuitousness of this is suggested in the opening exchange: ' "Evie, dearest girl, why aren't you in Yorkshire?" "No - motor smash - changed plans - father's coming." ' (82) The following chapter opens: 'The funeral was over'. (83) Mrs. Wilcox is dead; and the reader has received one of Forster's self-conscious 'shocks'. But in a novel which has set up a character like Mrs. Wilcox as a sort of spirit, who must anyway *physically* retire in favour of Margaret, the sense of contingency is strong - especially when the next chapter reveals Mrs. Wilcox's 'odd' will in which she has left Howards End to Margaret. The

Wilcoxes do not honour the will, and Margaret does not know of the bequest until the last page of the novel. Nevertheless, we sense that she will inherit the house (as she does). The question is: how will it come about? The Wilcoxes and the Schlegels move apart. Two years pass.

One evening, just as Margaret is thinking 'of the people who are really poor' (106), Helen bursts in with the news of a visit from, it transpires, Mrs. Bast, who has chanced on a visiting card Margaret had given Leonard well over two years before, and who has come to investigate what she assumes is 'another woman'. Leonard himself arrives the next evening to explain and later that same evening, as the sisters are sitting on the Embankment after a soirée, the following slightly improbable scene occurs:

> 'Did you say money is the warp of the world?'
> 'Yes'.
> 'Then what's the woof?'
> 'Very much what one chooses,' said Margaret. 'It's something that isn't money - one can't say more.' . . .
> 'For you?'
> 'Now that we have to leave Wickham Place, I begin to think it's that. For Mrs. Wilcox it was certainly Howards End.'
> *One's own name will carry immense distances. Mr. Wilcox, who was sitting with friends many seats away, heard his, rose to his feet, and strolled along towards the speakers. . . .*
> 'I believe we shall come to care about people less and less, Helen. The more people one knows the easier it becomes to re-place them. It's one of the curses of London. *I quite expect to end my life caring most for a place.*'
> *Here Mr. Wilcox reached them.* (122-3. My Italics)

The connection between the two families is re-established. In the ensuing conversation, it is Leonard Bast who is discussed, with Henry offering his fatal 'advice' about the Porphyrion Insurance Company: the connections are being rigorously forged. When Leonard visits the Schlegels the following Saturday, the Wilcoxes chance to arrive as well. After this the Basts disappear for a while, but the relationship between Margaret and Henry develops quickly. When Margaret is searching for a house it is Henry who helps her, and then proposes marriage. It is clear that Margaret is, in several ways, becoming Mrs. Wilcox's heir. A little later, when Margaret and Henry visit Howards End, it is contrived, because of forgotten keys (although it transpires that the door is not actually locked), that Margaret should enter the house alone and be 'mistakenly' greeted by Miss Avery as 'Mrs. Wilcox'. Evie's wedding takes place shortly after this and it is here that Helen arrives bringing with her the two Basts, who are now approaching total ruin as a result of Henry Wilcox's careless information about the Porphyrion. Henry accidentally meets Jacky in the garden, and the amazing 'connection' between them is revealed in Jacky's significantly *stagey* exclamation: ' "If it isn't Hen!" ' (216).[6] Jacky was Henry's mistress when he was abroad many years ago and so it is now apparent that he has, quite separately, 'ruined' both Leonard *and* Mrs. Bast. There follows a bridge passage, the main function of which is to remove Helen to her strange exile in Germany. Readers, as well as protagonists, are kept in suspense - a significant device for a writer who is working towards a dénouement.

The final movement opens with the strange scene in which Margaret (she and Henry have been quietly married in the meantime) again visits Howards End on her own ('Tibby promised to accompany her, but at the last moment begged to be excused' (248)) and finds that the odd Miss Avery has furnished the house with the Schlegels' effects which were being stored there. (The symbolic significance of this is inescapable). The finale proper begins with the plan to trap Helen, who is returning to England but does not want to be met, at Howards End in order to discover her 'secret'. This is developed as a typically Wilcoxian affair but it is also used by Forster to reinforce the suspense, and thus the emotional intensity of the conclusion. Helen is discovered to be pregnant: by Leonard Bast. (How this has come about is not explained until much later.) The novel then cuts back to the Bast story revealing how Leonard had glimpsed Margaret in St. Paul's a short time before, (her visit to the cathedral has been given an insignificant mention in the story some forty pages earlier) and decided to go and see her. The fact that he traces her to Howards End at exactly the time of Helen and Margaret's chance reunion there, only points to the increasingly artificial, even melodramatic, plotting of the book towards the end. This artificiality is compounded by the arrival, at precisely the same moment, of Charles Wilcox; by Leonard's death; and finally by Charles' conviction for manslaughter: 'It was against all reason that he should be punished, but . . .'

(311). The novel ends, of course, with the Wilcox family agreeing to their father's intention of leaving Howards End to Margaret, thus fulfilling Mrs. Wilcox's will. Dolly sums up the whole situation: ' "It does seem curious that Mrs. Wilcox should have left Margaret Howards End, and yet she gets it, after all." ' (318) Curious indeed.

A plot analysis of this kind clearly diminishes the overall complexity of the novel. Nevertheless, it illustrates how 'connection' is Forster's *donnée*, and how the plot is manipulated to achieve the pre-conceived end. His own comments on 'Plot' are apposite here:

> Sometimes a plot triumphs too completely. The characters have to suspend their natures at every turn, or else are so swept away by the course of Fate that our sense of their reality is weakened.
> . . . .
> The plot, then, is the novel in its logical intellectual aspect: it requires mystery, but the mysteries are solved later on: the reader may be moving about in worlds unrealized, but the novelist has no misgivings. He is competent, poised above his work, throwing a beam of light here, popping on a cap of invisibility there, and (*qua* plot-maker) continually negotiating with himself *qua* character-monger as to the best effect to be produced. He plans his book beforehand: or anyhow he stands above it, his interest in cause and effect gives him an air of pre-determination. (*AN*.100-3)

But since the ideological, as well as the structural, base of *Howards End* is 'connection', any sense of the tyranny of the plot reflects on the quality of the vision it is attempting to express. Probably the most intrusive instance of this in the novel is the 'connection' between Henry Wilcox and Jacky Bast. One can see why Forster needs it. It reveals the sordid 'secret life' of the 'public man'; it is a further instance of Henry Wilcox's disregard of other people; it enables Forster to suggest symbolically how destructive Wilcoxism is of poor but 'real' men (Henry effectively 'ruins' Leonard through ruining Jacky, as well as by his bad advice); it tightens up the sense of the interaction of the 'classes'; it leads on to Margaret's final 'victory' over the spirit of Wilcoxism; and perhaps most importantly, it offers the *necessary* justification for the final resolution. For 'the child' to inherit Howards End, it is essential for Helen to have a brief affair with Leonard; and the exposure of the Jacky/Wilcox relationship is used as a direct psychological explanation for behaviour it would have been difficult to effect 'realistically' in any other way, given Helen's character and social *mores*. But none of this alters the fact that, revealed late in the work, the extraordinary coincidence works back through the novel undermining the credibility of Forster's world and of other 'connections' more solidly achieved. Moral pattern has been achieved at the expense of a substantial world. It is striking how the intrusion of a fictional device can destroy the illusion of realism; and how the moral vision itself is then called radically into question. If this is *necessary*, one asks, and yet incredible, how is the vision valid?

By far the most melodramatic results of the vision's control of the plot, and of the need for fictive devices to bolster its uncertainty, are Leonard's death and Charles Wilcox's consequent conviction for manslaughter. Bast's death is presented in the following manner:

He entered a garden, steadied himself against a motor-car that he found in it, found a door open and entered a house. Yes, it would be very easy. From a room to the left he heard voices, Margaret's amongst them. His own name was called aloud, and a man whom he had never seen said, 'Oh, is he there? I am not surprised. I now thrash him within an inch of his life.'

'Mrs. Wilcox,' said Leonard, 'I have done wrong.'

The man took him by the collar and cried, 'Bring me a stick.' Women were screaming. A stick, very bright, descended. It hurt him, not where it descended, but in the heart. Books fell over him in a shower. Nothing had sense.

'Get some water,' commanded Charles, who had all through kept very calm. 'He's shamming. Of course, I only used the blade. Here, carry him out into the air.'

Thinking that he understood these things, Margaret obeyed him. They laid Leonard, who was dead, on the gravel; Helen poured water over him.

'That's enough,' said Charles.

'Yes, murder's enough,' said Miss Avery, coming out of the house with the sword. (302)

The whole passage is an extremely interesting technical operation. Forster intensifies the events by placing the earlier parts of the scene in Leonard's consciousness and, at the same time, avoids the overt melodrama which direct third-person narration would certainly have introduced. Even so, he achieves a degree of tension which gives the scene a powerful emotional and symbolic aura: the 'stick' is 'very bright' and acquires an apocalyptic quality (only later do we understand that Charles has used the Schlegel family sword, the symbolic import of which is unclear); the 'hurt' (the word has 'epic' associations) Leonard receives is in 'the heart', with all its metaphorical associations, not in the shoulders where he is struck (only later do we learn that he actually died of a heart-attack); books fall on him, suggesting again how he is stifled by 'culture' (this is later 'explained' by the fact that Miss Avery had placed the sword on top of the bookshelf). The phrase 'Leonard, who was dead' is another instance of Forster's shock technique and the scene closes with the spuriously 'significant' utterance of the sibylline Miss Avery. The whole effect is further heightened by Forster cutting back (in the following chapter) to the events preceding it. The question presents itself: Why does Leonard have to die at all and particularly in this melodramatic manner? The answers are related to the exigencies of the 'vision' and its formal expression. Leonard has to die to clear the way for his son to be 'Liberal England's' heir untrammelled by the drab reality of his father's life and class; Leonard himself would not fit into 'Howards End/England' but the child, brought up in the right environment, will. And Helen could not credibly have married a Bast. This is implicit in a conversation the sisters have near the end of the book; Helen says: ' "I ought to remember Leonard as my lover . . . . I tempted him, and killed him, and it is surely the least I can do. I would like to throw out all my heart to Leonard on such an afternoon as this. But I cannot. It is no good pretending. I am forgetting him." ' A little later, Margaret says:

'Don't fret yourself, Helen. Develop what you have; love your child. . . . I can't have you worrying about Leonard. Don't drag in the personal when it will not come. Forget him.'
'Yes, yes, but what has Leonard got out of life?'
'Perhaps an adventure'.
'Is that enough?'
'Not for us. But for him.' (314-5)

Pragmatic of Margaret this may be, but the double standard and the nonchalant tone, suggest just how little Leonard *himself* is regarded. As for Helen - 'Leonard seemed not a man, but a cause'

(290) - so perhaps for Forster. A further reason for the dramatic treatment his death receives is that it 'ennobles' him, and so makes the child's heredity more suitable for his symbolic role as the future of England. Finally, the drama of the scene helps to obscure the structural necessity of Leonard's removal: the 'vision' cannot contain the prosaic reality of his life and class, but he *can* be contained as the martyred dead. This is effectively confirmed by Margaret's meditation after his death:

> To what ultimate harmony we tend she did not know, but there seemed great chance that a child would be born into the world, to take the great chances of beauty and adventure that the world offers. She moved through the sunlit garden, gathering narcissi, crimson-eyed and white. There was nothing else to be done; the time for telegrams and anger was over, and it seemed wisest that the hands of Leonard should be folded on his breast and be filled with flowers. Here was the father; leave it at that. *Let squalor be turned into Tragedy*, whose eyes are the stars, and whose hands hold the sunset and the dawn. (307-8, my italics)

It is characteristic of Forster's dilemma in *Howards End* that he slips into vague and poetical rhetoric at points where the paradoxes of his vision obtrude. The point is that only by an idealisation of reality can the 'inner life' assimilate the 'outer'. The triumph of 'values' is not only wishful but implausible.

Charles Wilcox's conviction for Leonard's manslaughter is, in some ways, just as melodramatically handled, and is just as revealing. An awareness of what is to happen is planted gradually in the text, but the actual presentation of it is held for maximum effect:

> 'Have you realized what the verdict at the inquest will be?'
> 'Yes, heart disease.'
> 'No, my dear; manslaughter.'
>   Margaret drove her fingers through the grass. The hill beneath her moved as if it was alive.
>   'Manslaughter,' repeated Mr. Wilcox. 'Charles may go to prison. I dare not tell him. I don't know what to do - what to do. I'm broken - I'm ended.'
>   No sudden warmth arose in her. She did not see that to break him was her only hope. She did not enfold the sufferer

in her arms. But all through that day and the next a new life began to move. The verdict was brought in. Charles was committed for trial. It was against all reason that he should be punished, but the law, being made in his image, sentenced him to three years' imprisonment. Then Henry's fortress gave way. He could bear no one but his wife, he shambled up to Margaret afterwards and asked her to do what she could with him. She did what seemed easiest - she took him down to recruit at Howards End. (311)

What is again apparent is that these events are necessary to the pre-conceived scheme of the book and the emotional intensification is there to disguise the strains in the mechanism. The search for completion and harmony demands contingency; and Leonard's death and Charles' imprisonment successfully resolve problems which have been created by more sensitive and realistic perceptions in other parts of the novel. Forster had attempted to establish solidly the types of which the Wilcoxes and the Basts are examples. With the Wilcoxes he was particularly successful but (like the reality they represent) they became increasingly difficult to accomodate in the vision. The key line in the passage above, is: 'She did not see that to break him was her only hope'. The only way to pull Henry (his important economic resources and the house) into 'connection', and so realise the vision, was to 'break' him, to make him a shuffling, enfeebled, old man. One way of achieving this (for it is Forster's problem as much as Margaret's) is to send Charles to gaol on a manslaughter charge. It is necessary for the victory of the vision, and thus it is necessary in the plot. Henry's obtuseness, which blocks Margaret's attempts to expand his spirit and 'connect', is exorcised by the final smash. What sort of victory this constitutes for the vision's values, it is hard to say. Henry's spirit is not expanded, as Margaret earlier hoped (see above, p.84) it is merely broken. And it is broken, we must realise, by *the logic of the Wilcoxes' own attitudes*, not by the efficacy of Margaret's: Charles *must* attempt to sort out the family crisis in his tough, masculine way; he *must* horsewhip Leonard; and, having contributed to his death, 'the law, *being made in his image*, sentenced him to three years' imprisonment'. Margaret's liberal-humanism, except in a circumstantial way, has nothing to do with 'breaking' Henry; and Charles, the most consistent, recalcitrant and virulent

'Wilcox', is, like Leonard, simply removed, *hors de combat*. The vision goes its own way, but it is *given* certain essential free passes, with the result that neither the Basts nor the Wilcoxes are really included in 'Liberal England'. Forster is almost recognising this when he allows Margaret to say, looking back over 'the black abyss of the past': 'They had crossed it, always excepting Leonard and Charles' (313) And when she finally possesses Howards End, she muses: 'There was something uncanny in her triumph. She, who had never expected to conquer anyone, had charged straight through these Wilcoxes and broken up their lives'. (318) 'Uncanny' indeed and Forster himself obliquely supplies the explanation in his remarks on 'endings' in *Aspects of the Novel*: 'there is this disastrous standstill while logic takes over the command from flesh and blood. . . . No wonder that nothing is heard but hammering and screwing. . . . The novelist has to labour personally, in order that the job may be done to time'. (102-3) What remains at the end of *Howards End* as a result of the personal labour of the novelist, the hammering and screwing, is the situation - achieved but unrealised - which is necessary for the success of the original 'vision': an emasculated Mr. Wilcox, a motherly Helen, a Margaret approaching the numinous spirituality of Ruth Wilcox, and 'the child', unformed, unknown to the reader, to be taken on trust as the ultimate and rightful 'heir' of England. All we know is that he does not, significantly, suffer from hay-fever.

My last remark introduces a second aspect of Forster's 'fictional' technique, his symbolism. I do not intend to describe the significance of the separate symbols themselves in any detail - much of that is explicit in the description of *Howards End's* pattern and theme discussed above; I merely wish to indicate the way in which Forster *uses* symbolism. Symbolism can act as an intensification of objective situations, as verbal signs of an already existing state of affairs; Dickens and Shakespeare tend to use it in this way. It can also be archetypal, either anthropological or literary. In both of these cases, it is referential to more or less objective and commonly accessible phenomena. However, it can also be a private language, given internal currency by reiteration and context, but with a largely personal infrastructure. This sort of symbolism helps to *create* pattern, to point up significances and to express areas of experience which seem to evade prosaic statement. It also gives a kind of 'public', 'objective', status to essentially private and individual perceptions. It is here, of course, that the potential dangers lie: objects and actions can be given significance that they do not necessarily have, or they may be the products of a dream, imprecise and arbitrary but imbued with an aura of definition and certainty. This, I believe, is what Forster effects in *Howards End*, by his use of houses, hay and hay-fever, the wych-elm, country and city, and so on, and indeed by the entire symbolic action of the book. George H. Thomson[7] has argued that Forster does not borrow existing myths and symbols, as the modernists do, to impose order on flux; rather that he creates his *own* highly charged mythology and symbolism. But the argument is incomplete: Forster, we may agree, *does* create a personal symbolism but he uses *that* to impose pattern and order on his material. The question is: What is the significance of such symbols? Howards End is a house; why should it be 'England', except that Forster requires it to be so? And why does he require it to be so? Because it evokes a highly subjective vision of what he would like England to be: 'it was English, and the wych-elm that she saw from the window was an English tree'. (192) 'London', in the same terms, clearly fails to be 'English'. So many of the symbols in the book are, in effect, personal beliefs given an 'objective' significance but beyond the terms of the 'vision', they help to define nothing. Hay, for example, is an iterative symbol in the book, but it merely distinguishes those of the Mrs. Wilcox camp (the 'inner-life' characters) from those who are not - the other Wilcoxes and Tibby, all of whom suffer from hay-fever. It has no inherent significance, and its resonance is nil; it merely becomes schematic short-hand. We know, at the end, that Helen's son does not suffer from hay-fever, which means that he is one of 'the right sort'; but what his merciful freedom from hay-fever tells us about the future of England, it is more difficult to say.

In his essay, 'Ibsen the Romantic' (1928), Forster suggests that the power of Ibsen's symbolism springs from the fact that 'it is in the exact place which its surroundings require' (*AH*.84), and that 'a connection is found between objects that lead different types of existence; they reinforce one another and each lives more intensely than before'. (83) Forster's own symbolism is both more artificial and less resonant than Ibsen's. Interestingly enough, it is with Ibsen that Virginia Woolf compares Forster when she is discussing his symbolism, ('In this combination of realism and mysticism his closest affinity is, perhaps, with Ibsen'), but she suggests that where in Ibsen's work the sudden symbolic radiance of the ordinary object hits us with absolute certainty, in Forster's 'we are puzzled, worried. What does this mean? we ask ourselves. What ought we to understand by this? And the hesitation is fatal. For we doubt both things - the real and symbolical'. (*CEI*.346-7) Virginia Woolf suggests, wrongly I think, that it is because he is too much the realist. Rather, it seems to me, it is because the 'vision' demands a kind of expression which realism cannot accommodate. Nevertheless, she is absolutely right to point out the mutually damaging effect of the mixed modes of the book.

My overall point, however, is that the vision, at its most equivocal, requires just such an indefinite and insubstantial symbolism to find expression. Forster's remark, quoted earlier, about the 'tragedy' of life being 'that no device has been found by which these private decencies can be transmitted to public affairs', is revealed in its literary form by his own practice here. Private values are given public application by the use of symbolism, and this is nowhere better revealed than in the whole action of the novel which, as we have seen, is itself symbolic. The process of 'connection' and inheritance which is the basic movement of the book is perfectly acceptable at the individual and personal level, but it is intended to contain much wider public significance and to be about the fate of England. It is at this level that the system of 'connections' breaks down. Private solutions are not inevitably public solutions, as Forster was well aware: 'But in public who shall express the unseen adequately?' he asks in *Howards End*. (77) He might have answered that novelists, with their 'illusion of permanence' for Love at the end of their books (*AN*.62-3), attempt it, and especially if they employ an affirmatory symbolism like his own in *Howards End*. The problem is that the gap between the symbolic expression of his vision and the situation to which it is supposed to refer is too great, even for fictional 'transmission'.

One further example of Forster's private symbolism will lead us to the last major feature of the fictional embodiment of the vision. It is Helen Schlegel who uses the phrase 'panic and emptiness' to describe the inner life of the Wilcoxes, and it is Helen who is supposed to programmatise Beethoven's Fifth Symphony in Chapter V. 'Panic and emptiness' and 'the goblin footfall' are, however, used as motifs in the novel as a whole. It is as though the novelist has borrowed the private musings of one of his characters, and turned them into an objective symbolism. But it raises a larger point than this: the identity of the narrative voice itself in *Howards End*. Helen clearly 'thinks' the interpretation of the symphony. The passage is encapsulated by references to her, and in the middle Forster's stage-direction: 'Her brother raised his finger' (33) confirms that Helen is still the registering consciousness. And yet the recurrent use of phrases from it in other parts of the novel, *outside* Helen's consciousness, together with the last sentence of the passage: 'and that is why one can trust Beethoven when he says other things,' which is clearly the narrative, and not the dramatic voice, implies that it is Forster speaking too. Now if there is an unclear distinction between dramatic and narrative voices, then the overall tone of a book becomes personalised. Leavis noted the tendency in Forster's style many years ago: 'Mr. Forster's style is personal in the sense that it keeps us very much aware of the personality of the writer, so that even where actions, events and the experiences of characters are supposed to be speaking for themselves the turn of phrase and tone of voice bring the presenter and commentator into the foreground'.[8] The problem here is that if characters like Helen and Margaret, who are supposed to be living their lives autonomously, are no more than cyphers in the pervasive subjectivity of the novel, then the ostensibly objective support they should give to the visionary idea is again diminished. They are intended, after all, to make the vision 'real', but if they are indistinguishable from the narrative voice and the controlling vision, they are *only* real within its own terms, and the self-fulfilling tendency we have noticed before again obtrudes. Like Hardy's characters, as Forster saw them, they are too controlled by the demands of the vision to develop into free individuals who would confirm the reflections of the narrative voice. George Eliot, in her novels, is the wise woman who steps in to comment but her role is clearly defined and separate - an intelligent interpreter of the scene she surveys. Jane Austen holds the ironic veil firmly between herself and the characters she purports to identify with. But in Forster's case, subject and object, action and commentary are blurred, so that everything in the novel seems to be controlled by the novelist's own ideas.

This is especially so in the case of Margaret, who is certainly nearest to representing Forster although she is presented as an autonomous character who is supposed to develop in the course of the book. There is, of course, immediately a problem of verisimilitude here: how can a character who 'grows' throughout a novel, be at the same time a consistently reliable mouthpiece? In a sense, there is no problem: Forster and Margaret are so close, that the latter's 'growth' is merely a confirmation of the vision and even when she is 'judged' by the author (as, for example, over the 'trap' for Helen) it is entirely within the code of values to which she herself adheres. Time and again there is an ambiguity as to which 'voice' is speaking. For example, when Margaret takes Mrs. Wilcox Christmas shopping, we have the following piece of reflection:

> How many of these vacillating shoppers and tired shop assistants realized that it was a divine event that drew them together? She realized it though, standing outside in the matter. She was not a Christian in the accepted sense; she did not believe that God had ever worked among us as a young artisan. These people, or most of them, believed it, and if pressed, would affirm it in words. But the visible signs of their belief were Regent Street or Drury Lane, a little mud displaced, a little money spent, a little food cooked, eaten, and forgotten. Inadequate. But in public who shall express the unseen adequately? It is private life that holds out the mirror to infinity; personal intercourse, and that alone, that ever hints at a personality beyond our daily vision. (77)

Initially, Forster enters Margaret's mind and offers her reflections on the Christmas scene but by the end of the passage the tone is clearly that of the narrator. This movement effectively turns the private responses of an individual character in a particular situation into statements which purport to be general truths. In this case, London and the Christmas shoppers ('these people') are implicity judged as being without 'private life', not, finally, by Margaret, but by Forster himself. The London which is supposedly being strained through Margaret's consciousness is treated by the author as though it were the objective reality, and because his consciousness is almost identical to hers, London appears as it has to appear for the personal values of the vision to be confirmed.

This is the constant tendency of the novel: a vision affirmed by Art. The life that Forster might observe would scarcely support his vision of 'England'; but before the Great War, for a man of Forster's persuasion, there was still the possibility of believing in Liberal England victorious. For Forster, as for Margaret, (again their voices blend) Howards End and its wych-elm were potent evidence of the truth and viability of the vision: 'Their message was not of eternity, but of hope on this side of the grave.' (192) The fact that for public expression 'their message' required fictional manipulation is only further evidence of how complex an historical construct *Howards End* is.

At the very end of the novel, occurs the following well-known passage:

> 'There are moments when I feel Howards End peculiarly our own.'
>
> 'All the same, London's creeping.'
>
> She pointed over the meadow - over eight or nine meadows, but at the end of them was a red rust.
>
> 'You see that in Surrey and even Hampshire now,' she continued. 'I can see it from the Purbeck Downs. And London is only part of something else, I'm afraid. Life's going to be melted down, all over the world.'
>
> Margaret knew that her sister spoke truly. Howards End, Oniton, the Purbeck Downs, the Oderberge, were all survivals, and the melting-pot was being prepared for them. Logically, they had no right to be alive. One's hope was in the weakness of logic. Were they possibly the earth beating time?
>
> 'Because a thing is going strong now, it need not go strong for ever,' she said. 'This craze for motion has only set in during the last hundred years. It may be followed by a civilization that won't be a movement, because it will rest on the earth. All the signs are against it now, but I can't help hoping, and very early in the morning in the garden I feel that our house is the future as well as the past.' (316)

In a sense, this passage contains the essence of the whole novel: the conscious ambivalence of Forster's recognition of imminent breakdown and, at the same time, the affirmation of the vision ('the earth beating time'), despite that recognition. But it also acts as a commentary on the mode of the novel as a whole: Margaret's 'hope' in 'the weakness of logic' is reflected in the 'weakness of logic' in the fabric of the book. And that, in its turn, is symptom and sign of the weakness of logic in the vision. Paradoxically, the structural weaknesses are the result of the intense control exercised by Forster, and by the very completeness of the 'connections'. Time and again, to achieve them, Forster has to fall back on 'illogical' fictional devices which claim exemption from the laws of probability while their medium purports to be the phenomenal world of Edwardian England. But Forster, before the war made his Georgian utopianism totally untenable, could attempt to effect a solution which diminished the reality of his world while still employing techniques which cause that world to be inescapably intrusive. There is a constant tension, therefore, between the sketchy, under-realised, but potent 'reality', and the fictional attempts to realise the 'vision'. And this results from the tension between an admission that 'it is impossible to see modern life steadily and see it whole' (152), and the affirmation that 'in these English farms, if anywhere, one might see life steadily and see it whole.' (250) The former represents the realistic perception, the latter the contrived resolution. As the liberal-humanist world-view lost potency, so did the cosmography of the realistic novel seem to become redundant. For Forster, in the pre-war days of Liberal England, it could not substantiate the visionary dream; for later writers, in the post-war world, it could not express a seemingly unreal reality. The emphasis is, of course, very different, but the implication is the same: traditional realism was the expression of an assured and self-confident liberal-humanist world-view. The primary ambivalence of *Howards End* is its uncertainty of form. It is this tension which confirms its 'historical' significance, symptomatic as the novel is of the 'liberal crisis' - ideological and literary.

CONCLUSION: FORSTER AND THE 20TH CENTURY

Howards End, I have argued, is 'history from within' both at the conscious level, where the author explores a particular historical situation (usually his own), and at the unconscious level, where the novel reveals ambivalences in its representation of the world through its own formal structures. In these terms, *Howards End* is both a book of its time, and also prophetic. What it prophesies, I have suggested, is the crisis of liberal-humanism in the 20th century and, correlative to this, the crisis of realism in the novel. The former Forster consciously and bravely confronted, after the First World War, in his essays and broadcasts. His recognition of the latter may account for his decision not to write any more fiction after *A Passage to India.* But in both cases, the problems which *Howards End* identifies have been insistent in the post-war world.

It would be factitious to try and relate *Howards End*, and Forster's example, directly to 'tendencies', 'movements' or even to individuals active in literature in the post-war period but as a tentative, additional 'context' for what I have been saying, it is worth mentioning very briefly, a few writers whose work suggests that Forster's signposts were pointing somewhere. Virginia Woolf herself, believing as passionately in the irreducible importance of 'personal relations' and 'Art' as Forster, experimented continuously beyond the 'realistic' mode in order to express her vision, and to create objects of order and harmony which would hold the destructive element at bay. And D. H. Lawrence, who also recognised a strong affinity with Hardy, and whom Forster himself admired as a novelist of 'Prophecy', struggled to affirm 'life-values' against a rampant materialism in forms which broke radically with realism. Indeed many of his later short stories and novellas are consciously fabular, *The Virgin and The Gypsy* perhaps most successfully reconciling the claims of realism with those of the fable. More significant, in some ways, is the example of several of the younger writers in the 1930s, when the crisis of conscience for liberals was most overt and most acute: opposed to Fascism, they were averse to joining the Left and yet recognised that if they did not join they were effectively aiding and abetting Fascism. One of the classic fictional representations of this dilemma is in Rex Warner's novel *The Professor* (1938), which is unequivocally a fable; and it was Warner, significantly, who was later to write the British Book Council's pamphlet on Forster. In this, it is interesting to note, he expresses surprise that Forster 'should have chosen the novel form in which to expound his views'; but he nevertheless emphasises and admires Forster's use of the 'symbolic or allegorical method', his use of 'improbable' events for effect, and his 'elaborate symbolisms'.[1] Warner's earlier novel, *The Wild Goose Chase* (1937), an outrageously surreal fable, expounds his own socialist vision. But *The Aerodrome* (1941), where he is returning to a more humanistic position, combines fable and realism in a rather unhappy mix. Significantly, this was his last work of fiction. What Warner's case certainly suggests is that traditional realism could not serve the psychological or abstract ideological apprehensions of his time; and Edward Upward confirms this. Upward, who, according to Christopher Isherwood, discovered Forster's 'tea-tabling' approach to novel-writing ('the completely new kind of accentuation') while reading *Howards End*,[2] used fantasy and fable in the fiction he produced during the later '20s and early '30s (see *The Railway Accident* and *Journey to the Border* especially). These expressed, first, his neurotic sense of horror and breakdown, and second, his own vision of the socialist solution. But ultimately total commitment to politics and a 'vision' stopped him from writing fiction at all; presumably the terms in which to express it were lacking. He has recently returned, in his *In the Thirties* trilogy, to a flat autobiographical realism. Finally there is Christopher Isherwood, who acknowledges his debt to Forster in *Lions and Shadows*, and who clearly borrows the 'tea-tabling' approach in his Berlin stories to capture the hag-ridden atmosphere of Germany in the early thirties. It is worth remarking, in passing, that Isherwood's use of the ostensibly insouciant comedy of private life for a large and serious purpose is in some ways more successful that Forster's, precisely because it is not promoting a vision but specifically refers to a pressing social reality, the rise of Nazism.

To attempt to push 'connections' with Forster any further - to the 'new Gothic' of the American 'fabulators', for example - would be out of place and increasingly spurious. Suffice it to say that *Howards End*, at a number of levels, reveals post-war problems in Edwardian terms. And it remains a significant achievement; its gaps, tensions and uncertainty, themselves contribute to its continuing vitality and to its interest as 'history from within'.

In an essay on English prose between the wars, Forster wrote:

> Prose, because it is a medium for daily life as well as for literature, is particularly sensitive to what is going on, and two tendencies can be noted: the popular, which absorbs what is passing, and the esoteric which rejects it, and tries to create through art something more valuable than monotony and bloodshed. (*TC*.288)

Howards End contains both 'tendencies': it has 'absorbed what is passing' and it is also an attempt to 'reject it' and affirm through art a vision which Forster thought 'valuable'. Art, after all, was one of his main claims for humanity, and it represented for him a bulwark against dissolution. It is for this reason that he admired Beethoven so much, and why the final sentences of Helen's 'interpretation' of the Fifth Symphony in *Howards End* are so resonant:

> The goblins really had been there. They might return - and they did. It was as if the splendour of life might boil over and waste to steam and froth. In its dissolution one heard the terrible, ominous note, and a goblin, with increased malignity, walked quietly over the universe from end to end. Panic and emptiness! Panic and emptiness! Even the flaming ramparts of the world might fall.
>
> Beethoven chose to make all right in the end. He built the ramparts up. He blew with his mouth for the second time, and again the goblins were scattered. He brought back the gusts of splendour, the heroism, the youth, the magnificence of life and of death, and, amid vast roarings of a super-human joy, he led his Fifth Symphony to its conclusion. But the goblins were there. They could return. He had said so bravely, and that is why one can trust Beethoven when he says other things. (33)

This might well be a statement about Forster, too, and particularly in *Howards End*. He built the ramparts up, but he knew the goblins were there. We may perceive, now, how undermined and shot-through those ramparts are and were, but nevertheless they were built 'bravely' and *Howards End* itself - a fine liberal-humanist novel - was part of the process.

NOTES

Chapter 1. Introduction: Fiction as History

1. The lines are from Matthew Arnold's poem 'Stanzas from the Grande Chartreuse' (1867). Forster described Arnold admiringly as 'a prophet who has managed to project himself into our present troubles'. (*TC*.201)

2. Thomas Carlyle, 'On History' (1830), in *Selected Writings*, ed. Alan Shelston, Penguin Books, 1971, p.55.

3. Raymond Williams, *Modern Tragedy*, Chatto and Windus, 1966, pp.101-2. But see the whole of Part II, Chapter One.

4. *The Novelist at the Crossroads and other Essays* . . . , Routledge, 1971. In the later quotations here, Lodge is outlining Scholes' and Kellogg's case in *The Nature of Narrative*, Oxford University Press, 1966, but he generally subscribes to it himself.

Chapter 2. 'The Condition of England', 1900-14.

1. George Dangerfield, *The Strange Death of Liberal England*, (1935), Paladin, 1970.

2. John Colmer's *E. M. Forster, the Personal Voice*, Routledge, 1975, was published after I had written my own book, and so his chapter on *Howards End*, which also regards it as a 'Condition of England' novel, and which also relates it to Masterman, would seem to confirm my view. In fact, Colmer makes little of the Masterman connection (he refers mainly to *From the Abyss* (1903) anyway), and he has an almost totally different approach to the novel, barely treating it, in the end, as an 'historical' statement at all. He also skates very quickly over the problem of mode: 'How does Forster accommodate the Infinite and the Unseen in a "Condition of England Novel"?' (p.105). This he answers by simply borrowing two of Forster's own formulations in *Aspects of the Novel* 'Rhythm' and 'Prophecy' - and saying that Forster uses them in *Howards End*, 'thus accommodating the Infinite to social criticism'. (p.107) Which begs a great many questions!

3. In Lucy Cohen, *Lady de Rothschild and her Daughter*, 1935.

Quoted in *Edwardian England*, ed. S. Nowell-Smith, Oxford University Press, 1964: Chapter 1, Roger Fulford, 'The King', p.3.

4. Leonard Woolf, *Beginning Again, 1911-18,* Hogarth Press, 1964, p.44.

5. The quotations, in order, are from T. E. Hulme,*Speculations,* ed. Herbert Read (1924), Routledge paperback, 1960, pp.79-81, p.118, p.35, p.80.

6. Journal, 25, March 1914. In Charles Ricketts, *Self-Portrait,* collected by T. Sturge Moore and edited by Cecil Lewis, 1939, p.189.

7. *op. cit.*, p.134.

8. The phrase is C. E. Montague's in *Rough Justice* (1926), Chatto and Windus, 1969.

9. H. G. Wells, *Mr. Britling Sees It Through*, 1916, pp.46-7.

10. See, particularly, the Introduction to his *The Downfall of the Liberal Party, 1914-35*, Collins, 1966.

11. *op. cit.*, p.77.

12. Quoted in Christopher Hassall, *Edward Marsh,* Longman, 1959, pp.173-4.

13. The quotations, in order, are from his conclusion, 'The Aftermath', in *The Rise of European Liberalism*, (1936), Unwin Books, 1971, pp.157-8, p.170, p.160.

14. Nicholas Mansergh, *The Coming of the First World War,* 1949, p.171.

15. Osbert Sitwell, *The Scarlet Tree,* (1946), The Reprint Society, 1947, pp.241-2.

16. A. L. Baldry in *The Studio*, Vol.53, August 1911, p.175.

17. In a paper on John Masefield in November 1912. Reproduced in C. H. Sorley, *The Letters of Charles Sorley*, 1919, p.37.

18. Arnold Bennett, *Books and Persons*, 1917, p.92 and pp.49-50.

19. H. G. Wells,*Ann Veronica* (1909), Dent: Everyman, 1949, p.8.

20. E. J. Hobsbawn, 'The Fabians Reconsidered' in *Labouring Men* (1964), Weidenfield, 1968.

21. In 'Mr. Bennett and Mrs. Brown', *Collected Essays*, I, 1966, p.320.

22. These quotations are, respectively, from Wyndham Lewis, *Blasting and Bombardiering*, 1937, p.35, and from Lewis's Foreword to the Redfern Galleries Retrospective Exhibition catalogue, 1949.

23. From 'A Lecture on Modern Poetry' (written 1908-9, revised 1914). Reproduced, Michael Roberts, *T. E. Hulme*, 1938, Appendix II.

24. To Alice Corbin Henderson, October, 1913, *The Letters of Ezra Pound (1907-41)*, ed. D. D. Paige, Faber, 1951, pp.60-1.

25. *Beginning Again, op. cit.*, p.34.

26. *Blasting and Bombardiering, op. cit.*, p.40.

27. All the peoms quoted below are from *Georgian Poetry I* (1912) or *Georgian Poetry II* (1915), both edited by Marsh and published from The Poetry Bookshop.

28. Letter of February 1913, quoted by Hassall in *Edward Marsh, op. cit.*, p.208.

29. In *New Bearings in English Poetry* (Chatto and Windus, 1932), Peregrine, 1963. See for example, pp.14, 19, 48.

Chapter 3.   Forster and the Liberal Dilemma

1. *The Rise of European Liberalism, op. cit.* See respectively pp.167, 169, 156, 168, 158.

2. Matthew Arnold, *Culture and Anarchy* (1869), Cambridge University Press, 1971, pp.11 and 69.

Chapter 4.   Forster and the Novel

1. Spring (?) 1915. Quoted in Furbank's introduction to the Penguin *Maurice*, p.9.

2. *ibid*, p.8.

3. Thomas Hardy, *Jude the Obscure*, (1895), Macmillan, 1964, p.348.

Chapter 5.   Howards End: Fiction as History

1. Forster cut a passage which contained the comment: 'That is

the importance of Howards End, or of any scene that the reader may hold dear. It is poetry, while London is culture. It is not a movement, for it rests on the earth.' This would have followed the second paragraph of p.249 in the Penguin edition. Did Forster delete it because he did not wish his 'symbols' to break too heavily through the 'realistic' texture? See Oliver Stallybrass (ed), *The Manuscripts of Howards End*, 1973, p.275. This book is generally most useful for understanding the construction and intended 'meaning' of *Howards End*.

2. From 'Sonnet to a Friend'.

3. It is interesting that, later in life, Forster changed his attitude to London to a certain extent. See 'London is a Muddle' (1937) in *TC*, especially p.359.

4. Other critics who have been concerned with the duality of mode in Forster's work are: F. R. Leavis, *The Common Pursuit*, Chatto and Windus, 1952; Lionel Trilling, *E. M. Forster*, Hogarth Press, 1944; J. B. Beer, *The Achievement of E. M. Forster*, Chatto and Windus, 1962; C. B. Cox, *The Free Spirit*, Oxford University Press, 1963; Alan Wilde, *Art and Order: A Study of E. M. Forster*, New York, 1964; Frederick C. Crews, *E. M. Forster: The Perils of Humanism*, Princeton, 1962; George H. Thomson, *The Fiction of E. M. Forster*, Wayne State University Press, 1967. The problem with several of these works is that they are 'positive' readings, and attempt to explain away, or justify by special pleading, the tensions in Forster's work. Wilde's essay on *Howards End*, Cox's, and the end of Crews', however, tend to support my reading of it.

5. Lionel Trilling, *E. M. Forster*, Hogarth Press, 1944, p.22.

6. It is significant that Forster had considerable trouble with this scene, and indeed with this line in particular, as the manuscript suggests. See Stallybrass, *op. cit.*, pp.236-7.

7. In *The Fiction of E. M. Forster*, Wayne State University Press, 1967. The whole of this book is such special pleading that it tends, unfairly, to confirm one's sense of Forster's aesthetic and ideological uncertainties.

8. F. R. Leavis, *The Common Pursuit*, 1952, p.275.

Chapter 6.   Conclusion: Forster and the 20th Century

1. Rex Warner, *E. M. Forster*, 'Writers and their Work' pamphlets, Longman for the British Book Council (1960), pp.9, 13, 18, 22.

2. Christopher Isherwood, *Lions and Shadows* (1938), Four Square Books, 1963, p.107.

READING LIST

Forster's six novels are published by Edward Arnold. They are:

Where Angels Fear to Tread	1905
The Longest Journey	1907
A Room With A View	1908
Howards End	1910
Maurice	(completed 1914, revised 1959-60, posthumously published 1971)
A Passage to India	1924

There are two volumes of short stories:

The Celestial Omnibus	1911
The Eternal Moment	1928

The *Collected Short Stories* are published by Sidgwick and Jackson. They were first published in one volume in 1947.

Forster also wrote many essays, travel books and memoirs. Of these the most important, in our context here, are the essays collected in *Abinger Harvest* (1936) and *Two Cheers for Democracy* (1951); and *Aspects of the Novel* (1927). Forster's writings are now being edited by Oliver Stallybrass for Edward Arnold's 'Abinger' edition of the complete works, which will contain much hitherto unpublished material. As I have indicated in a note, one already published volume in this edition, *The Manuscripts of Howards End* (1973), is essential reading for a study of the novel.

There is, as yet, no full-scale biography of Forster, although an authorised one is being prepared by P. N. Furbank. Many of the major critical books about Forster of course contain biographical material; and of these one might mention K. W. Gransden's introductory study, *E. M. Forster* (Oliver and Boyd, 1962); J. K. Johnstone's *The Bloomsbury Group: A Study of E. M. Forster, Lytton Strachey, Virginia Woolf, and their Circle* (Secker, 1954), which is a most useful 'background' book anyway; and Wilfred Stone's large and symbolist/psychological study, *The Cave and the Mountain: A Study of E. M. Forster* (Stanford University Press, 1966).

There is now a very large amount of criticism of Forster's work. Philip Gardner's *E. M. Forster: The Critical Heritage* (Routledge, 1973) offers a useful selection of early responses and later criticism; and Malcolm Bradbury (ed), *E. M. Forster: A Collection of Critical Essays* (Twentieth Century Views, Prentice Hall, 1966), contains several good essays along with the editor's own introduction.

The following list of recommended secondary reading is highly selective, and includes general studies of Forster (which invariably have separate chapters on *Howards End*), and essays, either general or particular, which seem to me to offer interesting perceptions about that novel:

Virginia Woolf   'The Novels of E. M. Forster', in *Collected Essays*, I, Hogarth Press 1966. Still the most brilliant and suggestive of short studies of Forster.

Lionel Trilling   *E. M. Forster*, Hogarth Press, 1944. Revised Edition, 1967. Essential reading. Trilling understands Forster's 'liberal imagination' so intimately and writes about it so subtly, that this book seems to belong to Forster's own work rather than to the bulk of critical commentary.

F. R. Leavis   'E. M. Forster', in *The Common Pursuit*, Chatto and Windus, 1952. A sensitive and acute assessment of Forster which attempts to explain the ambivalent quality of his achievement.

Frederick C. Crews   *E. M. Forster: The Perils of Humanism*, Princeton University Press, 1962. A useful study, especially of Forster's location in the tradition of nineteenth-century liberalism and in early twentieth-century Cambridge thought. As with many Forster critics, however, there is a tendency in Crews' analysis of the novels towards special pleading.

C. B. Cox	*The Free Spirit: A Study of Liberal Humanism in the Novels of George Eliot, Henry James, E. M. Forster, Virginia Woolf, Angus Wilson*, Oxford University Press, 1963. An interesting general book - perhaps overgeneralised at times. The chapter on Forster usefully places him in a tradition, but does not push specific perceptions far enough.
Alan Wilde	*Art and Order: A Study of E. M. Forster*, New York University Press, 1964. A good study, which makes a serious attempt to see Forster's vision enacted in his formal structures, especially as a conscious aesthetic strategy. The chapter on *Howards End* I found most sympathetic.
John Beer	*The Achievement of E. M. Forster*, Chatto and Windus, 1962. Relates Forster's work to a romantic tradition. Is particularly interesting on Forster's visionary technique, arguing that his 'realism' is used successfully to curb his 'inward vision'. This is well argued, but not, I think, totally convincing.
James McConkey	*The Novels of E. M. Forster*, New York: Shoe String, 1957. Again concerned with the visionary in Forster. Most useful because it reads Forster's works against his own formulations ('Prophecy', 'Rhythm', etc.) in *Aspects of the Novel*.
John Colmer	*E. M. Forster: The Personal Voice*, Routledge, 1975. The most recent full-length study of Forster. Interesting because it deals with material released after Forster's death, and for its sensitive reading of the novels. But see my note 2 Chapter 2, for a comment on Colmer's section on *Howards End*.